THE COMPLETE HISTORY OF AMERICA (abridged)

by

Adam Long, Reed Martin and Austin Tichenor

JOSEF WEINBERGER PLAYS

LONDON

THE COMPLETE HISTORY OF AMERICA (ABRIDGED)
UK edition first published in 2006
by Josef Weinberger Ltd
12-14 Mortimer Street, London, W1T 3JJ
www.josef-weinberger.com
general.info@jwmail.co.uk

ISBN 0 85676 284 9

Printed by Commerical Colour Press plc, Hainault, Essex, England

IMPORTANT NOTE

The use of the name "REDUCED SHAKESPEARE COMPANY"
in any way whatsoever to publicise, promote or advertise any
performance of this script is EXPRESSLY PROHIBITED.

Likewise, any use of the name "REDUCED SHAKESPEARE
COMPANY" within the actual live performance of this script IS
ALSO EXPRESSLY PROHIBITED.

The play must be billed as follows:

THE COMPLETE HISTORY OF AMERICA (abridged)

by

Adam Long, Reed Martin and Austin Tichenor

ABOUT THE AUTHORS

Adam Long. Adam lives in a little house in north London with his wife Alex, his son Joe, their friend John, and a stray cat who regularly attacks every member of the family. Adam is the proud holder of a British driver's license. He cites his influences as Harpo Marx, Dogen Zenji, and the Grateful Dead.

Reed Martin has co-authored four other plays with The Reduced Shakespeare Company – THE BIBLE: THE COMPLETE WORD OF GOD (abridged), and THE COMPLETE MILLENNIUM MUSICAL (abridged), ALL THE GREAT BOOKS (abridged) and COMPLETELY HOLLYWOOD (abridged). He has also contributed additional material to THE COMPLETE WORKS OF WILLIAM SHAKESPEARE (abridged). He has written for the BBC, National Public Radio, Britain's Channel Four, RTE Ireland, Public Radio International, the Washington Post, and Vogue magazine. Prior to joining the Reduced Shakespeare Company, Reed was a Clown and Assistant Ringmaster with Ringling Brothers/Barnum & Bailey Circus. He has a BA in political science/theater from UC Berkeley and an MFA in acting from UC San Diego. He lives in Northern California with his wife and sons.

Austin Tichenor. For the Reduced Shakespeare Company, Austin is also the co-author of the stage plays THE BIBLE: THE COMPLETE WORD OF GOD (abridged), THE COMPLETE MILLENNIUM MUSICAL (abridged), ALL THE GREAT BOOKS (abridged), COMPLETELY HOLLYWOOD (abridged); the half-hour TV film *The Ring Reduced,* and the radio productions of *The Reduced Shakespeare Radio Show* (BBC), The Reduced *Shakespeare Company Round Table* (NPR's All Things Considered), and *The Reduced Shakespeare Company Christmas* (Public Radio International). He is also author of over twenty plays and musicals for young audiences, including DANCING ON THE CEILING, (an adaptation of Kafka's *Metamorphosis*), THE FIRST OLYMPICS, and the musicals STONE SOUP and RIVER TOWN. He is a member of the Dramatists Guild.

The Writers would like to thank: Dee Ryan, Jane Martin, Mike McShane, David Stafford, Rick Reiser, Matt Croke, American Repertory Theatre, Jess Winfield, and Scott Ewing for their contributions to the development of the script. Lobsters to the Firesign Theater.

THE COMPLETE HISTORY OF AMERICA (ABRIDGED) was originally produced and performed by the Reduced Shakespeare Company. It had its first public performance on 18 March 1993 at the Stewart Theatre at North Carolina State University. Later that year it was performed at the American Repertory Theatre in Cambridge, MA, the Lincoln Center "Serious Fun" Festival in New York City, and the Montreal "Just for Laughs" Festival. With one cast change, the play had extended runs at the Kennedy Center in Washington, DC, in the summers of 1994 and 1995. With two cast changes the play opened at the Criterion Theatre in London's West End in 1996, where it ran continuously until 2005.

ORIGINAL CAST

Adam Long
Reed Martin
Austin Tichenor

KENNEDY CENTER CAST

Matthew Croke
Reed Martin
Austin Tichenor

ORIGINAL LONDON CAST

Matthew Hendrickson
David Letwin
Adam Long

FOR WHAT IT'S WORTH

Although we use the names Adam, Reed, and Austin within the script, each cast member should use his own real name when performing the show.

There are a number of topical references in the script. The humour and relevance of these will fade over time, so we encourage each production to change these references to keep them as up-to-date as possible. This is not to say that scenes may be rewritten (which is, in fact, strictly prohibited) but rather we are giving you permission to change a dated punch line or reference from 'Kato Kaelin' to 'Paris Hilton', or from 'Lyndon Johnson' to 'George W Bush'.

The production elements described in the script are from the original production by the Reduced Shakespeare Company. Consequently, the scenery, props, and costumes were all "reduced" in both quality and number. You will not be so encumbered, and may be tempted to use real explosions, live animals, and leggy showgirls. This sounds like fun but might falsely raise audience expectations.

It has been our experience that the script works best when performed seriously. That is to say, the script is funny so play it straight. But most of all, have fun and perform the show with energy and pace. To give you a general idea of the pace: when we performed the show, the first act ran about fifty minutes, the second act about forty-five minutes. Sometimes, if the audience actually laughed, the show was known to run an extra 17 seconds.

ACT ONE

The set consists of two elements. Against the black upstage drop there is a long illustrated timeline depicting people and events from 1492-2000. It is broken up in the middle by a large American flag, which hangs vertically UC. It is not the American flag with fifty stars currently in use, but the original flag with thirteen stars in a circle. The audience hears the following recorded announcement.

AUSTIN　　(*voice over*) Ladies and gentlemen, The Complete History of America (abridged) will begin shortly. The animals used in tonight's performance were tortured under the strict supervision of the American Humane Association. The actors in tonight's performance are proud to wear Nike®, the Official Footwear of the complete history of America. Nike®. Just do it. And management wishes to remind you that this theatre is equipped to provide assistance to the hearing-impaired. If you or a member of your party is hearing . . . paired . . . eeze . . . tact . . . nush . . . for more . . . nkyou. And now, for your edification and entertainment, The Complete History of America (abridged).

　　(*The boys enter from the back of the auditorium, singing. They are dressed smartly in slacks and dress shirts and, perhaps, coats and ties. ADAM beats on a toy drum, REED crashes cymbals. They march to the stage, singing the melody perfectly in three-part harmony but with the words themselves two counts off the beat.*)

ALL　　OH SAY CAN YOU SEE BY
THE DAWN'S EARLY LIGHT WHAT
SO PROUDLY WE HAILED AT
THE TWILIGHT'S LAST GLEAMING WHOSE
BROAD STRIPES AND BRIGHT STARS THROUGH
THE PERILOUS NIGHT O'ER
THE RAMPARTS WE WATCHED WERE

SO GALLANTLY STREAMING AND
THE ROCKETS' RED GLARE THE
BOMBS BURSTING IN AIR GAVE
PROOF THROUGH THE NIGHT THAT
OUR FLAG WAS STILL THERE, OH
SAY DOES THAT STAR-SPANGLED BANNER
YET WAVE O'ER THE
LAND OF THE FREE AND THE HOME
OF THE BRAVE.

REED   Good evening, ladies and gentlemen, I'm Reed
            Martin.

AUSTIN   I'm Austin Tichenor.

ADAM   I'm Adam Long, and welcome to tonight's
            performance of . . .

ALL   . . . The Complete History of America
            (abridged).

REED   Tonight we explore the history of a great
            nation. But before we do, I'm sure many of you
            are wondering, "Why? Why the complete
            history of America?" Well, I'm sure there are as
            many answers to that question as there are
            members of tonight's cast. Austin, why don't
            you start?

AUSTIN   Thank you, Reed, and in the tradition of my
            white Anglo-Saxon Puritan imperialist
            westward-expansionist capitalist intellectual
            forebears – I will be brief. I believe it was
            Benjamin Franklin who said, "History is written
            by the winners." Well, tonight it's our turn.
            Reed?

REED   Thank you, Austin. Adam?

ADAM   What?

REED   Well, would you like to explain why we're
            doing this show?

ADAM

Oh . . . well, all right. Before we started doing this show I didn't know too much about American history, so I started to read up on it – you know, like in books 'n stuff. And I took a ton of notes. I must have written like three pages of notes, front and back. And I found a quote about what history is that I thought was totally cool. It said, "History is the deconstruction of necessary illusions and the study of emotionally potent oversimplifications." And that still holds true today because I see this show as about remembering. Remembering the past. Because it's like that old saying: "Those of us who forget the past are doomed to, you know, forget other things, like your car keys, or even your own phone number." So I see this show as like a Post-It note on the refrigerator of America. A Post-It note that says, "Hey, America! Don't forget to Tivo American Idol tonight!" 'Cause it's only through remembering our past that we can learn from our mistakes, or at least blame them on somebody else, and then move on, into a better future. An enlightened capitalism, perhaps. Free of all forms of racism, sexism, ageism, weightism, hair-colorism, making-funism, and Godism. And you may say that I'm a moron, and I say to you, yes. But I'm a moron with a dream, and that, my friends, is the most dangerous kind of moron.

REED

Thank you, Adam. That was . . . whelming. Let me see if I can crystallize for you why exactly it is we're doing the Complete History of America. In fact, I think it's very simple. Some time ago we received a letter from a ten-year old girl named Amy who lives in Warwickshire, England. Amy writes . . . (*He takes out the letter and reads.*) "Dear guys, I think it would be fun for you three Americans to condense all of English history, because you three are so hysterical and handsome and intelligent and wise. Love and kisses, your fan forever, Amy." Well, Amy, this is the kind of letter that pisses

us off! Did it occur to you that maybe we have
no interest whatsoever in English history?
Why can't Americans do American history?
Where do all you English get off with this
cultural superiority complex?

ADAM   We've got a culture, too, y'know, and a
            history.

REED   Yeah, and it may not be as long as yours but
            it's like my mother always said, "It's not the
            length of your history, it's what you've done
            with it."

AUSTIN   And when we looked into it, we realized that
            many Americans are at best uninformed or at
            worst embarrassed about our own history.

REED   Well, dammit, we've got nothing to be
            embarrassed about! We brought the world its
            first democracy and man on the moon and Mark
            Twain and . . .

AUSTIN   And Paris Hilton.

REED   Yeah! And Paris Hilton! And McDonald's and
            Coca-Cola and Big Bird and Bart Simpson so
            don't go telling us we don't have a culture and
            a history, little smarty pants Amy!

AUSTIN   So hang on, Amy, we got a lot to accomplish in
            the next ninety minutes.

ADAM   Let's do it!

            (*They come together for a high-five.*)

ALL   Go . . . US!

            (*Blackout. Lights up on* REED.)

REED   We begin at the beginning: 1492 Spain! The first
            chapter of the history of America is about to be
            written by that legendary Italian explorer . . .

(ADAM *enters and blows a toy horn fanfare.*)

REED/ADAM   . . . Amerigo Vespucci! (ADAM *exits.*)

REED   We join him now in his humble map shop on the Spanish dockyards.

(REED *exits as* AUSTIN *enters, in the garb of a 15th Century Italian, carrying a Chianti bottle and a map. Remember what we said about playing it straight? In this scene we used bad Italian accents and flamboyant stereotypical hand-gestures . . . but we did it very seriously.*)

AUSTIN/   Ring-a! Ring-a! (*Answering his hand.*) Hello,
VESPUCCI   Maps-R-Us, Amerigo Vespucci here . . . What? Have we got maps?! We're the map mavens! What are you looking for? . . . A sea route to India? What are you, nuts? I got your sea-route to India right here, buddy . . . (*He takes a swig from the Chianti bottle.*)

ADAM/   (*offstage*) Amerigo!
SOPHIA

(AUSTIN *spits his wine [actually water] out onto the audience.* ADAM *bursts into the room dressed as Sophia Vespucci.*)

ADAM/   Amerigo Vespucci!
SOPHIA

AUSTIN/   Shaddup, woman! I'm on the telephone! (*Into
VESPUCCI   phone.*) Look, buddy, I . . . (*He hangs up.*) Great! You just lost me a customer. I hope you're happy, Sophia!

ADAM/   You know what would make me happy? If – just
SOPHIA   once – when I sent you out for food you didn't come back with fish!

(*She slaps him with a large stuffed fish.*)

AUSTIN/   But Sophia, this is God's food!
VESPUCCI

ADAM/   Don't give me that line about holy mackerel.
SOPHIA   I'm sick of it.

AUSTIN/   But I get a good deal on mackerel.
VESPUCCI

*(If your theatre is situated so that you can see
the audience clearly from the stage, and if
latecomers can be seen entering by a majority
of the crowd, then now's the time for some fun.
Arrange it so latecomers aren't seated until
after* AUSTIN *spits on the audience.* ADAM *and*
AUSTIN – *carry on as best you can with the
scene until the inevitable distraction in the
audience becomes too much. Then* AUSTIN *can
yell,* "Sophia, who are these people you're
bringing into my living room?" ADAM *can then
respond:* "That's another thing, Amerigo –
every time we get into an argument, you have
friends over!" AUSTIN: "Oh, no, these are not
my friends! My friends would have been on
time!" *If you do it right, you should get
thunderous applause. Then you can ask them
where they were (and really get an answer –
it'll pay off later). You should also introduce
yourselves, which can bring* REED *on, angrily
demanding* "Where are they?" *The bit can end
quite nicely by telling them what they missed.*
ADAM *says,* "Well, you missed it when I said
'You may say that I'm a moron!' That was
pretty funny." REED *then says,* "And I said,
'It's not the length of your history, it's what
you've done with it.'" *Finally,* AUSTIN *should
march right up to the latecomers with his
bottle of Chianti, say,* "Well the only thing I
did was – " *and spit-spray a fine mist of water
all over them. Then get back onstage, say*
"Where the hell were we?" *and resume the
scene. Sure, the people you're picking on*

won't like it, but the rest of the audience will love it.)

ADAM/ SOPHIA	Well, we wouldn't need a good deal on mackerel if you sold a few more maps!
AUSTIN/ VESPUCCI	Pasta fazule spaghetti bolognese! Are you saying I'm a failure as a map maker?
ADAM/ SOPHIA	My parents told me not to marry you. They said, "Marry a nice boy, like that Christopher Columbus. He's going places!"
AUSTIN/ VESPUCCI	Well, maybe if I had a wife who gave me a little support every now and then.
ADAM/ SOPHIA	Oh, no! It's not my fault. Let's face it, Amerigo, nobody buys your maps because they're crap!
AUSTIN/ VESPUCCI	What do you mean, crap?
ADAM/ SOPHIA	What part of crap don't you understand?
AUSTIN/ VESPUCCI	I knew you'd say something like that. Here – take a look at this.

(AUSTIN *claps his hands.* REED *tosses an inflatable globe from the wings, which* AUSTIN *catches.*)

How do you like that, huh? I made it myself.

ADAM/ SOPHIA	Well, it might be fun in pools, but you don't know what you're doing. Every time you see a land mass, you name it the same thing.
AUSTIN/ VESPUCCI	No!
ADAM/ SOPHIA	No?! Alright, let's take a look. (*He refers to the inflatable globe.*) Now what's this? North America? Down here you've got South

Amerigo? But what about this . . . Union of
Soviet Socialist Vespucci? No, no, no. Besides,
Amerigo, everybody knows that the world is
flat.

AUSTIN/   Ha! I'm way ahead of you. Take a look at this.
VESPUCCI

(REED *tosses out a flat globe like a frisbee.*)

See? I made it shaped like a pizza pie!

ADAM/   Sacrobambino!! You are worthless, Amerigo!
SOPHIA   Worthless!!

AUSTIN/   I am not worthless! I am trying to make a name
VESPUCCI   for myself, that's all. I have a dream, which is
                 something you will never understand. I'm
                 sorry, Sophia, but I have to go.

(REED *enters, wearing his accordion. He hands*
AUSTIN *a ship's wheel for steering and places*
a conquistador helmet on AUSTIN'S *head.*)

I can't stay here any longer. I have to be
something! All that I can be!! Harry Verducci,
mi amore! I'm off to discover a larger world.
You will never see me again. (*Handing her the
Chianti bottle.*) When you drink that wine, and
eat this fish, remember me.

ADAM/   (*wailing*) Amerigo!!!
SOPHIA

(REED *vamps on a minor chord as the lights
blackout. A spotlight comes up on each of the
boys as he begins to sing.*)

REED   AMERIGO!!

AUSTIN   AMERIGO!!

ADAM   AMERIGO!!

ALL   HEY!

REED	AMERIGO VESPUCCI WAS HIS NAME
ADAM	VESPUCCI!
REED	CHARTING LAND MASSES WAS HIS GAME
ADAM	POOCHY-WOOCHY!
AUSTIN	NOT SCRABBLE OR PARCHEESI
ALL	NO! CHARTING LAND MASSES WAS HIS GAME!
AUSTIN/ VESPUCCI	I SET SAIL TO CHART THE SEAS IN 1499
ALL	IN A VESSEL FULL OF DREAMS PASTRAMI AND CHEAP WINE
REED	THE MATE WAS A MIGHTY SAILOR MAN
AUSTIN	THE SKIPPER BRAVE AND SURE
ADAM	AMERIGO SET SAIL THAT DAY FOR MORE THAN A THREE-HOUR TOUR
ALL	MUCH MORE THAN A THREE-HOUR TOUR
	(REED *hits three sustained chords while* AUSTIN *and* ADAM *hum underneath his following speech.*)
REED	In 1502, after two long, treacherous voyages, Amerigo concluded that what everyone had thought was India was actually a new world. He named it Mundus Novus – Latin for Giant Nose. Eventually it bore his name: AMERICA. History was made.
	(*The tune changes to "America the Beautiful."*)
ALL	AMERIGO! AMERIGO!

AUSTIN/ VESPUCCI	GOD SHED HIS GRACE ON ME!
ADAM/REED	YOUR NAME WILL LIVE FOREVER NOW
ALL	FROM SEA TO SHINING SEA! AMERIGO . . . AMERIGO . . . A-HAH!

(*Blackout.* AUSTIN *re-enters while* ADAM *rolls out a large flip-chart. The top page, facing the audience, says: "AMERICAN".*)

AUSTIN
And so, the new world was called "America." And we, the people of that land, were called "Americans." But what does it mean to be an American? Reed?

(ADAM *and* AUSTIN *find seats in the audience.*)

REED
Thank you, Austin. And thank you, Adam. Let's take a moment to look at this word, "American", shall we? It's just eight simple letters. But over the years this word has come to stand for Liberty, Equality, Prosperity, and the sort of gosh-darned persnicketiness that has made the US what it is today. Let's take a closer look, shall we? The first letter couldn't be simpler: just little ol' "A." But "A" is the first letter of the alphabet, isn't it? The first, the beginning, the progenitor of democracy, perhaps? "A" also means one, implying oneness, or unity, so you've got to admit, that "A" is one loaded little letter. Now the second three letters spell out "MER", which is the French word for . . . anyone?

(*Someone in the audience yells, "The sea!" Sometimes* ADAM *or* AUSTIN *will yell out "The sea!" if the audience won't.*)

That's right: the sea. In this case, obviously referring to the sea of humanity to which America brings Unity. And don't forget, that it

was across the sea that the French sent us the
Statue of Liberty, the symbol of freedom in the
midst of a SEA of oppression. In gratitude, we
later sent them Jerry Lewis. Now the last four
letters speak for themselves, don't they? They
spell out very plainly – say it with me now: "I
CAN!" Now you've got to admit, that's one
plucky word! Not many people know this, but if
you rearrange these eight letters just a little bit,
they spell out: . . .

(REED *reveals a new sign saying "I CAN
REAM," and signs are revealed for each of the
following phrases and anagrams.*)

. . . "I CAN REAM." Now, if you rearrange the
letters in the name of our very first president,
(*Reveals sign.*) GEORGE WASHINGTON, you
get (*Reveals sign.*) GAGGIN' ON WET HORSE,
which was actually the title of a popular song
at the time of the Revolution. And, if you
rearrange the letters in the name of Richard
Nixon's first vice-president (*Reveals sign.*)
SPIRO AGNEW, you get – (*Reveals sign.*) say
it with me now – GROW A PENIS. Ladies and
gentlemen, that's what it means to be an
"American." I thank you.

(*During the applause* AUSTIN *and* ADAM *come
back onstage.*)

ADAM   Now we know what little Amy is thinking at
this point. She's thinking, "Hey, they skipped
Christopher Columbus! That's not fair! He
discovered the New World and they hardly
mentioned him!" Nyah nyah nyah, nenenenene!

REED   Well, his name really wasn't Christopher
Columbus, it was Christobal Colón. And he
bumped into the New World by mistake. And
he wasn't even the first one here because the
Vikings, the Japanese, and the Irish were
probably here before him, and there was a

native population of over 90 million here before he arrived.

AUSTIN   Yeah, but in fairness to Columbus, though, he was the first man to slaughter and enslave the native population in the name of Christianity, and he became very wealthy in the process. So in that sense, he was the first true American. (*If someone applauds this sentiment,* AUSTIN *can misinterpret the reaction and say,* "Hey, some genocide fans here tonight! Cool!")

ADAM   Austin, I'm sorry but that is so Eurocentric.

AUSTIN   What do you mean?

ADAM   The story of the First People begins long before the European invasion of the native settlements in North America.

AUSTIN   That's true, but it doesn't fit on our timeline.

(REED *gets an idea and dashes into the wings.*)

ADAM   Well then the timeline is bogus.

AUSTIN   It's not bogus, it's just incomplete . . .

(REED *re-enters holding a rolled-up timeline extension. It depicts world events, real and fictional, between 10,000 BC and 1492.*)

REED   Hey, guys! Take a look at this.

AUSTIN   What's that?

REED   It's a supplementary timeline which I prepared earlier.

(ADAM *shakes his head in disgust and exits.*)

AUSTIN   Good thinking.

REED   It covers all historic events prior to 1492.

AUSTIN   Okay, I'll buy that. Create more of a "Big Picture" sorta thing.

(REED *starts unfurling the timeline and heads into the audience if he can.*)

All right, we're going back in time, ladies and gentlemen. Back to when the first people came to North America. Where are you now, Reed?

REED   Austin, I'm at the Crucifixion of Christ, and I can tell you I don't see Mel Gibson anywhere.

AUSTIN   Well, don't stop there. Keep going.

(REED *is by now unfurling the timeline up the aisle.*)

REED   Okay, Ancient Romans, Ancient Greeks –

AUSTIN   Toga, toga —

REED   Yeah, we're having an ancient kegger. Ancient Egyptians, invention of the written word, birth of Bob Dole . . . Austin, it's getting kinda cold back here.

AUSTIN   That's 'cause you're near the Ice Age, man. You better get back up here, you're not really dressed for it. That's far enough anyway. Ladies and gentlemen, we're about 12,000 years back now and scientists speculate that the first people came to North America across the Bering Straits between twelve and fifty-thousand years ago.

(ADAM *re-enters with a feather in his hair and sets a bowl of water, a maraca, and a tom-tom on the stage. Then he sits on the stage DC and stares straight at the audience.*)

ADAM   My people are not so interested in what scientists have to say. We have our own stories of how the world began.

AUSTIN   Ladies and gentlemen, we are indeed fortunate, because Adam is part Crow Indian. His great-grandmother was a fullblooded Crow . . .

REED   . . . and had a wing-span of eight feet.

ADAM   That is so typical of the white man.

AUSTIN   She was a full-blooded Crow *Indian*, and lived in the Pueblo Indian village of San Juan in the Rio Grande Valley. As his great-grandmother told him, Adam will now tell us the story of the First People.

            (AUSTIN *and* REED *sit on the stage, on either side of* ADAM, REED *with the tom-tom,* AUSTIN *with the bowl of water.* ADAM *attempts to begin his speech three times, but each time he is inadvertently interrupted by* REED *who is focussed on pounding the tom-tom.*)

ADAM   Cut it out! (REED *now taps lightly on the tom-tom.*) Yonder in the north there is singing on the lake. Cloud maidens dance on the shore. There we take our being. At the beginning of all beginnings all was water. To the North . . . was water. (*In turn,* AUSTIN *dips his hand into the bowl of water and flicks it to the four points of the compass, with the last flick directed at the audience.*) To the South . . . was water. To the East . . . was water. And to the west . . . you guessed it . . . more water. And so, the water was everywhere, and everything was totally wet.

            (AUSTIN *tosses the rest of the water out of the bowl and onto the audience. He then sits down and begins to shake the maraca in rhythm.*)

            How the water came to be, nobody knows . . .

            (REED *and* AUSTIN *stop playing.*)

REED   Okay, Adam, we get the water. Just get on with
              it!

ADAM   Hey, the water's important. It's archetypal. So
              back off. Okay. (*Trying to remember his place
              in the story.*) Okay . . . okay . . . water north,
              water south, everything wet. Okay, okay, okay!
              Now, living above the water there was a
              coyote, a duck, and . . . umm . . . another duck,
              and they walk into a bar!

              (REED *does a rimshot on his drum.* REED *and*
              AUSTIN *mutter disgustedly at the bad joke.*)

ADAM   No, I'm just kidding. Anyway, the coyote says
              to the ducks, "Dive down under the water and
              see what you can find." So the ducks dive
              down and come up with mud and roots. And
              the coyote spread the mud all around. He made
              the hills, mountains, valleys, hollows. And he
              planted the roots and grew up grasses, plants,
              trees. Then Coyote took a handful of mud and
              blew into it and made male animals and female
              animals. He made female ducks, which made the
              two ducks happy, I can tell you. And there was
              a great quacking and gnashing of feathers. And
              finally, Coyote made the first man and the first
              woman out of mud. And there was a great
              copulation . . . and it was good.

              (REED *and* AUSTIN *stop playing.*)

AUSTIN   Now at this point, doesn't the tribal elder
              usually perform a dance, Throwing Bull?

ADAM   Right you are, Wears Glasses To Look Smarter.
              At this point, the tribal elder performs Hiu!
              Hiu! He! He! He! I!

AUSTIN   What's that?

ADAM   That's a very holy dance. It's the dance of the
              Antelope's Intestine. As the Elder of this

group would you do the honors, Sits Down To
Pee?

REED

I'd be delighted.

(*NB: You may have actors who, unlike Austin,
are not optically-challenged. In London, they
used the following.*)

AUSTIN

(*who's been drumming a dog/tom-tom*) Doesn't
the tribal elder perform a ritual dance?

ADAM

Right you are Pounds on Dog . . . (*To* REED.) So
if you'd do the honors, Head Reflects
Sunlight?

REED

I'd be delighted, Has Strong Right Arm.

(*So go ahead – mix 'em up!*)

(REED *pulls a long uninflated balloon out of
his pocke*t. ADAM *takes his place at the tom-
toms.* REED *performs some sacred gestures with
the balloon.*)

ADAM

Okay, the Elder has his Intestine in hand and
the dance is ready to begin. First, the Elder
performs a dance of blessing. He asks blessing
on the corn, that it might be bountiful. He asks
blessing on the rain that it will be plentiful. He
asks blessing on the hunters, that they may be
brave and virile . . .

(REED *inflates the balloon. It's upright and
phallic.*)

REED

Eat your heart out.

ADAM

Now the Elder performs the Nine Ceremonial
Twists of the Antelope's Intestine. The first
three twists represent the star, moon, and sky –
the constant companions of the antelope. The
second three twists represent the father,

mother, and child – the family of the antelope;
and the final three twists represent earth, wind,
and fire – the favorite band of the antelope.
And finally the Elder brings forth the image of
the antelope!

REED   (*holding up a balloon dog*) Arf! Arf!

ADAM   Give it up for the tribal elder!

              (REED *presents the balloon animal to a person
              in the front row.* REED *and* ADAM *exit.*)

AUSTIN   Of course, after 1492 everything changed. In
              fact, in our research we discovered that the
              16th Century lasted a hundred years. And in
              that hundred years, America was crawling with
              famous explorers, mostly Spanish, whose ships
              could be recognized by the large fuzzy dice
              hanging from their masts.

              (Reed *re-enters.*)

REED   That's right, Austin. But did you know that it
              was actually an Englishman, Sebastian Cabot,
              who first set foot on the continent of North
              America? He later became very famous as the
              voice of Bageera the Panther in the Disney film
              The Jungle Book.

AUSTIN   And although it was the Portuguese Magellan
              who first circumnavigated the globe,
              Englishman Sir Francis Drake was the second
              man to do it when he discovered what is now
              San Francisco in his ship "The Golden Hind".

BOTH   Coincidence? You decide!

              (ADAM *enters.*)

ADAM   Hey, Austin, can I do that poem I wrote?

AUSTIN   Is it the one about Nantucket?

ADAM   No, I couldn't find a rhyme for it.

AUSTIN   Yeah, sure.

                       (AUSTIN *and* REED *shrug and exit.*)

ADAM   I wrote a poem about the first English
                       settlement in North America. This is my poem.

                       'TWAS 1607, IN THE FINE MONTH OF MAY,
                       THAT THREE PROUD SHIPS LANDED AT
                                          CHESAPEAKE BAY
                       AND A NEW LIFE BEGAN FOR GOD'S PEOPLE
                                          THAT DAY.

                       FOR JAMESTOWN WAS BORN,
                       SO THE STORY WAS TOLD,
                       TO SPREAD OUR LORD'S WORD
                       AND FOR MINING OF GOLD.

                       THE LIVIN' WAS HARSH FOR THOSE BRAVE
                                          MEN AND WOMEN.
                       THEY TOILED AND THEY SWEATED AND
                                          RARELY WENT SWIMMIN'.
                       THEY WHEEZED AND THEY GRUNTED AND
                                          SOILED THEIR LINEN.
                       THEIR CUPBOARDS WERE BARE, BUT THEIR
                                          CESSPOOLS WERE
                       BRIMMIN' WITH CESS.
                       OH, YES.

                       THE NEW WORLD WAS TAMED BY MEN
                                          WHO WERE BRAVE
                       AND MEN WHO WERE STRONG AND SIX
                                          MILLION SLAVES
                       AND INDENTURED SERVANTS AND THE
                                          IROQUOIS NATION
                       WHO GAVE UP THEIR LAND WITHOUT
                                          COMPENSATION
                       'CAUSE THE INDIANS LANDED
                                          UNDERNEATH PLYMOUTH ROCK
                       JOHN SMITH WAS A RAPIST, POCAHONTAS
                                          DIED OF SMALLPOX
                       AND THAT'S A FACT, JACK! HUNH!

GIVE IT AWAY, GIVE IT AWAY, GIVE IT
                                                     AWAY, NOW!
GIVE IT AWAY, GIVE IT AWAY, GIVE IT
                                                     AWAY, NOW!

SO THE PILGRIMS PERFECTED THE ART OF
                                                     GOOD LIVIN',
THEY CARVED UP THE LAND AND
                                   INVENTED THANKSGIVIN'
AND LICKETY SPLIT, JUST AS QUICK AS
                                                     YOU PLEASE,
WHAM BAM MA' AM THERE WERE
                                             THIRTEEN COLONIES

THERE WAS GEORGIA AND MARYLAND
                                     AND SHUT MY MOUTH
TWO KINDS OF CAROLINA BOTH NORTH
                                             AND SOUTH.
THERE WAS A BUNCH OF COLONIES THAT
                                   CALLED THEMSELVES NEW
LIKE YORK, JERSEY, HAMPSHIRE, AND
                                             DELHI, TOO.
VIRGINIA, CONNECTICUT, DELAWARE,
                                             RHODE ISLAND,
AND IT IS KNOWN
MASSACHUSETTS IS THE HOME OF MY
                                             MAN NOAM.

THAT'S N-O-A-M CHOMSKY
AT THE MASSACHUSETTS INSTITUTE OF
                                             TECHNOLOGY.

AND FINALLY PENN, WHICH IS THE
                                   QUAKER STATE,
SO BACK OFF BUDDY 'CAUSE THOSE
                                   QUAKERS WERE GREAT.
THEY THOUGHT THAT KILLING WAS
                         WRONG AND INTOLERANCE RUDE,
BUT TRY TELLING THAT TO THE PURITANS,
                                             DUDE.

(ADAM *exits. Lights up on* REED/PASTOR. *He wears a goofy hunting cap and a pastor's collar.*)

REED   Hello, and welcome to our dual weekly meetings of Salem's First Church of Tolerance and National Witch-hunter's Association. I'm your pastor, the Reverend Feral Orwell. A quick announcement before we get going here. Thursday is youth night here at the church. We'll play "Hangman" and "Pin the Blame on the Warlock", so bring your little demons along and we'll scare the hell out of them. You know, last night the Lord came to me in a vision and He said, "Reverend Feral Orwell, you and your followers need to kill 100 witches this week or I'm going to call you home." Well, I don't want to go home – you know what my wife is like – so I urge you to hunt the good hunt. And don't forget that this witch-hunt will begin an American tradition that will carry on well into the 21st century. Now, to avoid tragic cases of mistaken identity like we had last Halloween, here's how you spot a real witch. They melt when you throw water on them, they're surrounded by flying monkeys, and she's America's most famous homemaker who's been convicted of insider trading.

(AUSTIN *bursts in with scroll, wearing a tri-corn hat. He is a town crier.*)

AUSTIN   (*reading the scroll*) Hear ye, hear ye! This just in! We interrupt this witch-hunt to bring you the French and Indian War! French and British at war again, this time in North America! In sports, the Patriots trounce the Redskins.

(AUSTIN *runs off, handing the scroll to* ADAM *who has run on, also wearing a tri-corn hat.* REED *also wears a tri-corn when he enters.*)

ADAM   (*reading the scroll*) Oh, yea! Oh, yea! British and colonists defeat French and Indians. King

George celebrates victory by imposing taxes on tea, stamps, sugar, and anything else he can think of! Colonists are up in arms!

(ADAM *runs off.* AUSTIN *and* REED *run on.*)

AUSTIN   Hey, didja hear that?

REED   What?

AUSTIN   King George has raised taxes and the people are up in arms.

REED   Really! (AUSTIN *exits. To* ADAM, *who has run on.*) Did you hear?

ADAM   What?

REED   King George has raised taxes and the people are arming themselves!

ADAM   No way!

REED   Way! (*Exits.*)

ADAM   Wow! (*To* AUSTIN, *who has run on.*) Hey! The King has doubled our taxes and we're putting together a people's army to fight him right now. We're off to throw tea in the harbor!

AUSTIN   Uh, oh! Trouble's brewing!

              (AUSTIN *and* ADAM *run off, while* REED *bursts in reading the scroll.*)

REED   (*reading the scroll*) Oh, yay! Oh, yay! Big tea party in Boston! Dump tea in the harbor to protest taxes! Alice in Wonderland and Mad Hatter slated to attend!

              (AUSTIN *and* ADAM *run on. All three speak together.*)

AUSTIN   Peas and carrots, peas and carrots . . .

ADAM	Harumph, harumph, harumph . . .
REED	Rutabagas, rutabagas, rutabagas . . .

(ADAM *and* REED *exit.*)

AUSTIN (*reading the scroll*) Hear ye! Hear ye! British soldier kills Crispus Attucks – an African-American – in the Boston Massacre. Four others dead. The colonists are in revolt.

(AUSTIN *exits as* ADAM *and* REED *enter.*)

REED Hey! Did you hear?

ADAM What?

REED The colonists are revolting.

ADAM I know. Did you ever eat with one of 'em?

REED Doh!

(ADAM *and* REED *exit.* AUSTIN *runs on reading the scroll.*)

AUSTIN Oh, yea! Oh, yea! British attack at Lexington and Concord. Revolution underway. Paul Revere and the Raiders number one on the charts with "The British Are Coming".

(AUSTIN *exits.* ADAM *gallops on, riding an invisible horse.*)

ADAM Listen my children and you shall hear
Of the midnight ride of Paul Revere
He said with a grin
While wiping his chin
If my ear was a –

(AUSTIN *and* REED *dash on in time to say:*)

ALL BANG!

AUSTIN   I hear a shot!

ADAM   (*in a French accent*) I hear a shot, monsieur!

REED   (*in a Mexican accent*) I hear a shot, señor!

ADAM   (*in a Chinese accent*) I hear a shot, grasshopper!

AUSTIN   (*in a Russian accent*) I hear a shot, Comrade!

REED   I ear-hay an ot-shay, orky-Pay!

ALL   It was the Shot Heard 'Round The World.

REED   But the shot that started the American Revolution remains shrouded in mystery to this day. Nobody knows who pulled the trigger or why, but at the end of the day 73 people lay dead. Let's recreate for you now what happened on that fateful day at Lexington and Concord. Adam?

(ADAM *moves the flip-chart and reveals a large diagram, complete with buildings, arrows, and marching soldiers.*)

ADAM   Thanks, Reed. Now according to the Official Benedict Arnold Committee Report, a single bullet was fired from the fourth floor window of the Lexington and Concord Scroll Depository.

(ADAM *pulls an oversized bullet out his coat pocket and moves it across the diagram in the way he describes.*)

We have a mock-up of the bullet here. The bullet followed this trajectory, killing 17 soldiers who were marching in formation, then it pulled a U-turn, then turned right up Main Street. Austin?

(ADAM *hands the bullet to* AUSTIN.)

AUSTIN

Thanks, Adam. Now at this point the bullet, which we have marked with an 'X', (AUSTIN *turns the bullet to reveal that it is marked on one side with a red 'X'.*) killed four colonists before stopping here at the Tar and Feathers Tavern for lunch, where it killed an additional six people, smashed through a table, knocking it back and to the left – and took off in a white Ford Bronco without tipping the waitress. The bullet has never been recovered.

ALL

Coincidence? You decide!

(ADAM *and* REED *exit. The lights fade down to a single special on* AUSTIN.)

AUSTIN

And a full-fledged Revolution was under way. The colonists wanted to stop the British government from imposing unfair and exorbitant taxes so that the American government could impose unfair and exorbitant taxes. The commander-in-chief of the colonial army was George Washington, who commanded a tiny contingent of fighters known as the Minute Men: volunteer soldiers ready to do battle with a minute's notice. The Minute Men: brave patriots fighting for American liberty. The Minute Men: better lovers than you might think. It was the whole British Empire versus George Washington and his small army.

(*Lights up on* ADAM *and* REED *kneeling as two* MINUTE MEN, *still wearing their tri-corn hats. They also wear trench coats which conceal the fact that they are each holding two sticks with shoes at the ends. They appear to be four feet tall.*)

ADAM & REED

(*singing*)
WE REPRESENT THE LEXINGTON LEAGUE
THE LEXINGTON LEAGUE
THE LEXINGTON LEAGUE

AND IN THE NAME OF THE LEXINGTON
LEAGUE...
WE WISH TO WELCOME YOU TO VALLEY
FORGE!

(They curtsy. AUSTIN *enters in powdered wig,
aviator glasses, and corncob pipe, becoming
George Washington – but also looking a bit
like General Douglas MacArthur.)*

AUSTIN/ WASHINGTON	Gentlemen, gentlemen! I want to thank you for volunteering your services to this great cause, but I'm afraid I have some bad news. The road ahead is fraught with hardship and you are simply not what I had in mind.
ADAM/ MINUTE MAN 1	Waddaya mean?
AUSTIN/ WASHINGTON	I mean, I need regular, full-sized soldiers.
REED/ MINUTE MAN 2	Look, I hate to burst your bubble, mahogany-mouth, but we're exactly what you asked for.
AUSTIN/ WASHINGTON	Are not.
ADAM & REED/ MM 1 & 2	Are too.
AUSTIN/ WASHINGTON	Are not.
ADAM & REED/ MM 1 & 2	Are too.
AUSTIN/ WASHINGTON	Stop it!
ADAM & REED/ MM 1 & 2	Stop it!
AUSTIN/ WASHINGTON	And that's an order.

ADAM & REED/ And that's an order.
MM 1 & 2

AUSTIN/   I'm a stupid little soldier and I'm acting like a
WASHINGTON   child.

               (REED *and* ADAM *smile at each other.*)

ADAM & REED/ (*gleefully*) We know you are but what are we?!
MM 1 & 2

AUSTIN/   Doooh!
WASHINGTON

ADAM/MM 1   Low-five. (ADAM *and* REED *slap hands.*) Look,
               Cherry-tree Choppers, let's cut to the chase
               here. Do you recognize this piece of paper?

               (ADAM *hands* WASHINGTON *a piece of
               parchment, which he has pulled out of the
               inside of his tri-corn hat.*)

AUSTIN/   Uh-huh.
WASHINGTON

ADAM/MM 1   Is that your signature?

AUSTIN/   Yes.
WASHINGTON

ADAM/MM 1   Would you mind reading it to the audience?

AUSTIN/   All right. (*Reading.*) "Uncle Sam needs you.
WASHINGTON   Wanted: Mine-yoot Men to form colonial – "
               (*Beat.*) I could've sworn I said "minute men."

ADAM/MM 1   (*to the audience*) Even in its early days,
               America had a problem with literacy.

REED/MM 2   (*grabbing the paper and reading*) "Expel the
               Evil Empire from North America and meet
               chicks. High frostbite tolerance a plus. No tea

drinkers please. Be all that you can be. Apply
in person – Valley Forge."

AUSTIN/   Well, I'll be damned.
WASHINGTON

ADAM/MM 1   This is a clear case of Vertical Discrimination.

ADAM & REED/   (*various*) We'll sue! We'll sue! You can talk to
MM 1 & 2   my attorney. I'll see you in court!

AUSTIN/   Oh, all right all right, you have the job.
WASHINGTON

ADAM & REED   Yay! (*In unison, they wave their right fists in a
                circle five times.*) Whoop, whooop, whoop,
                whoop, whoop!

AUSTIN/   Now, gentlemen, here's the situation . . .
WASHINGTON

                (REED *and* ADAM *lean in to listen, each
                leaning both stick-legs off the ground in the
                opposite direction of the lean.*)

                Thousands of well-trained British soldiers
                using the most advanced weapons versus a
                ragtag band of undertrained colonists.

                (REED *and* ADAM *lean back to upright.*)

ADAM/MM 1   Are we that ragtag band?

AUSTIN/   Uh-huh.
WASHINGTON

ADAM/MM 1   That don't sound so good.

REED/MM 2   Why don't we just surrender now and save
                time and energy?

AUSTIN/   Look, I'm tired . . .
WASHINGTON

(AUSTIN *stomps his foot for emphasis. The two* MINUTE MEN *lift their false-feet briefly off the floor as if they are bounced into the air.* AUSTIN *doesn't pause, though, he goes right on.*)

. . . of all this sniping and insinuendo that our war effort is anything less than positively . . .

(AUSTIN s*tomps again.* MINUTE MEN *bounce again.*)

. . . impacting on the British defensive entrenchment situation. It is very difficult . . .

(AUSTIN *lifts his foot off the ground as if to stomp, but instead stands on one foot. As* AUSTIN *lifts his one foot, the* MINUTE MEN *both lift both of their feet off the ground and hold them there.*)

. . . to enumerate quantitatively at this junctive in time just how offensive our capabilities are. But I'll tell you one thing –

(AUSTIN *sets his foot down. The* MINUTE MEN *set their feet down.*)

. . . contraceptive to your popular belief, we're taking precautions at every penetration and by the grace of God, our upcoming thrust will break through the last membrane of British defense and into Virginia.

REED/MM 2   Will this make you the father of our country?

AUSTIN/   Well, I have cut through some cherry trees in
WASHINGTON   my time, to be sure. (*If the audience groans or boos at this,* AUSTIN/WASHINGTON *should stare them down and say,* "I cannot tell a lie!".) Now gentlemen, all we need now is a flag to rally 'round. Any ideas?

REED   Well, not many people know this, but when we
                    aren't Mine-yoot men we enjoy working with
                    fabric, colors, and design . . .

AUSTIN/   What the hell?!
WASHINGTON

                    (*During the previous two lines,* REED *and*
                    ADAM *have stepped up and out of their midget
                    attire, revealing fancy dresses or aprons
                    underneath.*)

REED/BETSY   Hi, I'm Betsy Ross and this here's my sister,
                    Diana.

ADAM/DIANA   Stop! We'd like to share with you our designs
                    for the new American flag.

AUSTIN/   Carry on.
WASHINGTON

REED/BETSY   (*putting a bonnet on his head. He indicates
                    the American flag that is part of the set*) Now,
                    I'm sure all of you know that this is the flag we
                    finally settled on. But along the way, a number
                    of flags were rejected for various reasons and
                    we'd like to share some of those with you.

                    (ADAM/DIANA *reveals the flags one-by-one on
                    the flipchart. The first is the British Union
                    Jack.*)

REED/BETSY   Rejected for obvious reasons. I'm sure many of
                    you are also familiar with the "Don't Tread On
                    Me".

                    (ADAM/DIANA *reveals "Don't Tread On Me".*)

REED/BETSY   The first design I came up with I really liked,
                    but turned out to be a little ahead of its time.

                    (*Something vaguely patriotic, but abstract
                    and Picasso-esque.*)

REED/BETSY   Then I struck upon an idea which I loved, that
                  captured the heart, the very essence of what
                  America is all about, but the founding fathers
                  rejected it as too commercial. Here it is.

                  (*This one reads: "I ♥ $".*)

AUSTIN/   Enough shilly-shally, ladies! Let's get out there
WASHINGTON   and kick some British butt!

                  (*The boys march in rhythm.*)

ADAM   Left! Left! Left left left!
                  So the rebel troops brought the Brits to their knees
                  By hiding themselves behind rocks, behind trees
                  In formation the British lined up to attack
                  They marched neatly in rows and got shot in
                                              the back
                  And finally in Yorktown in Fall, '81
                  The British surrendered – the Yankees had won!

ALL   Gimme an M!
                  Gimme an E!
                  Gimme an R! I! C!
                  Gimme an A!
                  Gimme an N!
                  Watzzat spell? 'MURRICAN!!!!

                  (REED *exits.* AUSTIN *and* ADAM *take pipes out
                  of their pockets.*)

AUSTIN/   Madison! Madison!
JEFFERSON

ADAM/   Jefferson! Jefferson!
MADISON

AUSTIN/   Madison, how about this as the beginning of
JEFFERSON   our new Bill of Rights? "Tax and Spend"?

ADAM/   No, no, too liberal. How about this? "Don't tax,
MADISON   but still spend"?

AUSTIN/   No, too conservative, I think. Here's what it
JEFFERSON   should be: "Whether you're a brother or
                  whether you're a mother, you're staying alive,
                  staying alive."

ADAM/ MADISON	No, that's too Seventies.
AUSTIN/ JEFFERSON	I suppose you're right . . .

(REED/FRANKLIN *enters wearing bald cap with long hair at the edges, and glasses.*)

REED/ FRANKLIN	No, no, gentlemen, focus, please.

(*If the audience laughs at his absurd wig,* REED/FRANKLIN *can say,* "Yeah, I know. I look like Bozo".)

How about this: "All men are created equal."

(*Beat. Then they laugh themselves silly and take a large toke off their pipes.*)

ADAM/ MADISON	This is great tobacco, Jefferson. Grow this yourself?
AUSTIN/ JEFFERSON	(*high-pitched voice*) Yesss – Monticello Gold. I've got the munchies. Do you suppose Dolly Madison has any more of those cakes?
ADAM/ MADISON	I can't believe the Bill of Rights is due tomorrow.
REED/ FRANKLIN	Now, as the world's first democracy, I think we should guarantee Freedom of Religion, Freedom of the Press, and Freedom of Speech.
ADAM/ MADISON	If you guarantee all those rights, people are going to be saying all kinds of crazy stuff and pissing each other off.
REED/ FRANKLIN	Well, then let's give everyone the right to carry a gun to shoot each other, and the right to a fair and speedy trial by a jury of their peers after they do. Are we in agreement?

ADAM/   Totally.
MADISON

AUSTIN/   Totally.
JEFFERSON

REED/   Cool. Now, I would also propose that we draw
FRANKLIN   up a Bill of Wrongs as a companion piece to
               the Bill of Rights. As I see it, Article One could
               forbid leaving toilet seats up. Article Two
               could forbid our gorvernment taking away our
               civil liberties in the name of homeland security.
               Article Three could forbid people we barely
               know from sending us 'amusing' e-mails, and
               so on. Are we in agreement?

ADAM/   Totally.
MADISON

AUSTIN/   Totally.
JEFFERSON

REED/   Cool.
FRANKLIN

ADAM   Now, before we go on, I want to say something
               about the Bill of Rights.

REED/   What's that, Madison?
FRANKLIN

ADAM   No, not as Madison, as me, Adam. I've been
               doing some thinking about this Bill of Rights
               thing and I find it problematic.

AUSTIN   What do you mean?

ADAM   I mean, they say we have free speech in this
               country, right?

AUSTIN   Right.

ADAM   So can I say anything I want?

AUSTIN	Yeah.
ADAM	No! Did you know the Supreme Court says I can't say ANYTHING I want?
AUSTIN	Like what?
ADAM	Classic example: you can't yell "fire" in a crowded theatre, right?
AUSTIN	Right.
ADAM	Well, what if there is a fire in a crowded theatre?
AUSTIN	Adam, that's not the point.
ADAM	What is the point?
AUSTIN	The point is that the First Amendment guarantees all Americans the full freedom of expression.
ADAM	Freedom of expression?! What is that, a joke?
AUSTIN	No . . .

(ADAM *works himself into a frenzy*.)

ADAM	Could I go on television and advocate the overthrow of the government?! No! In an R-rated movie, could I show a pair of lips kissing a nipple? No! You can show that same nipple being lopped off with a chainsaw, but you can't kiss it!
AUSTIN	That's gross!
ADAM	It's not gross! It's what I'm talking about! Oh! Okay, perfect – what'd you say, freedom of expression? (*Indicating the American flag upstage*.) Suppose I wanted to light this flag on fire right now. Could I?
ADAM/AUSTIN	No!

AUSTIN   Because it would be a fire in a crowded theatre!

               (*Beat.* ADAM *considers this.*)

ADAM   That's not the point.

AUSTIN   What is the point?

ADAM   The point is the system is suppressing my right
               to say what I want, when I want . . .

AUSTIN   You're saying exactly what you want right now
               and nobody's stopping you.

ADAM   Yeah . . . well . . . that's because I'm white and
               a male when I'd rather be black and a woman
               and feel my belly swollen with my baby, and be
               able to sing like Aretha Franklin! That's what
               I'm talking about, man. R-E-S-P-E-C-T! Oh,
               forget it . . .

               (ADAM *exits, crying. Beat.*)

REED   You hurt his feelings.

AUSTIN   No, I didn't.

REED   Yes, you did.

AUSTIN   Well . . . I don't care.

REED   Austin, you should apologize.

AUSTIN   Forget it! I'm not going to apologize. He was
               overacting.

               (ADAM *pokes his head onstage.*)

ADAM   No, he's right, Reed. I was overacting.

REED   Great! Get ready for the next scene – I'll
               introduce it.

(ADAM *and* AUSTIN *exit.*)

Let's see, we've covered about 50,000 years of American history in thirty-five minutes. Are there any questions? No? Okay, well think about it, save them up and in the second act we'll give you the chance to ask us any serious question about American history. But right now let's get back to the new country which more than doubled in size in 1803 when President Thomas Jefferson – by this time sober – purchased the Louisiana Territory from France for about $15 million, or roughly three cents an acre. He then sent Lewis and Clark west to explore this vast and uncharted area. Ladies and gentlemen, we are indeed fortunate tonight to have that fabulous team back with us. Just returned from their hugely successful tour of the western circuit – all the way from Bismarck, Boise, Clatskanie, Walla Walla, and Cucamonga – here they are! You know them, you love them, please bang your hands together for . . . Lewis and Clark!

(REED *leads the applause and exits.* ADAM/ LEWIS *and* AUSTIN/CLARK *enter doing a vaudeville two-step. They wear loud coats and carry canes.* AUSTIN *wears a coonskin cap.* ADAM *wears a skunkskin cap with an arrow through it. They sing. NB: See special note on copyright page.*)

AUSTIN/ADAM   HELLO EVERYBODY, BOY WE'RE GLAD TO
                                                BE HERE

AUSTIN/CLARK   JUST ME

ADAM/LEWIS   MYSELF

AUSTIN/ADAM   AND WE!

(*They turn upstage.*)

WE'RE GLAD TO BE BACK

(*They turn downstage.*)

WE'RE GLAD TO BE FRONT
WE'RE GLAD TO TELL YOU FACTS ABOUT
THIS WONDERFUL COUNTRY!

HELLO EVERYBODY BOY WE'RE GLAD TO BE
                                          HERE
WE'RE GONNA TURN YOUR DARK SKIES BLUE

ADAM/LEWIS   I'M WACKY, I'M ANTIC

AUSTIN/CLARK   I'M DASHING AND ROMANTIC

AUSTIN/ADAM   AND WE'RE GLAD TO BE WITH –

AUSTIN/CLARK   You know, Lewis, it's great to be here in . . .
                (*Insert name of the actual city here.*) Isn't this
                a beautiful audience?

                (REED *has re-entered UR with a table full of
                sound-making devices: cymbals, slidewhistle,
                and bike-horn. He uses them as indicated
                throughout.*)

ADAM/LEWIS   Yeah. 'Specially that guy there.

                (ADAM *points at a man in the audience.* AUSTIN
                *hits him with a large foam-rubber hammer.
                SFX: Cymbal crash.*)

AUSTIN/CLARK   Get back here. Settle down. Ladies and
                gentlemen, we just rode in from Oregon –

ADAM/LEWIS   And boy, are our butts tired!

                (*SFX: three horn honks, as* ADAM *grabs his
                own behind and hops three times.*)

AUSTIN/CLARK   We were sent out to explore the vast uncharted
                American wilderness.

ADAM/LEWIS   We traveled across deep mountains and high valleys, all the way to the ocean.

AUSTIN/CLARK   Be specific.

ADAM/LEWIS   Okay. The Specific Ocean.

(AUSTIN *hits him again with the hammer. SFX: cymbals.*)

AUSTIN/CLARK   C'mon, these people want details. We spent the winter of 1805 in North Dakota . . .

ADAM/LEWIS   Hey, Clark, what's the capital of North Dakota?

AUSTIN/CLARK   I don't know, Lewis. What is the capitol of North Dakota?

ADAM/LEWIS   About forty-seven cents!

(ADAM *grabs the hammer from* AUSTIN *and hits himself. SFX: cymbals. The audience inevitably responds poorly to this terrible joke.*)

AUSTIN/CLARK   Hmm, tough room. Anyway, we determined that the whole Louisiana Territory is ripe for plunder and penetration. The trick is knowing how to negotiate with the Indians.

ADAM/LEWIS   INDIANS?!

(ADAM *hops into* AUSTIN'S *arms.*)

AUSTIN/CLARK   No no, settle down. There are no Indians here. (AUSTIN *sets* ADAM *down.*) But in North Dakota we were fortunate enough to meet Sacagawea, our Indian guide and interpreter. She went all the way with us . . .

ADAM/LEWIS   Well, she didn't go all the way with all of us . . .

(*SFX: slide whistle as* ADAM *makes a crude pelvis-thrust gesture.*)

AUSTIN/CLARK   Stop it. That's disgusting. She was married to
                that French-Canadian trapper.

ADAM/LEWIS   I know, I know – (*As Jimmy Durante.*)
                Everybody's a Canadian! (*SFX: two horn
                honks. The audience groans or makes no noise
                at all.*) Well, they love that joke in Quebec.

AUSTIN/CLARK   But not in . . . (*Name of place where the show
                is being performed.*) . . . apparently. Sacagawea
                traveled with us all the way to the West Coast
                and back.

ADAM/LEWIS   She saved our lives more than once, our
                faithful Indian squaw. (AUSTIN *hits* ADAM *with
                hammer. SFX: cymbal crash.*) Hey! What's the
                matter?

AUSTIN/CLARK   I don't like that word.

ADAM/LEWIS   What word? Squaw? (AUSTIN *hits him again.
                SFX: cymbal crash.*) What's wrong with sq –
                that word?

AUSTIN/CLARK   It's demeaning and offensive. Don't you watch
                Oprah?

ADAM/LEWIS   No, I don't. What's it mean?

AUSTIN/CLARK   It's a Native American word which Anglo
                culture has appropriated and applied
                generically to all Indian women. It refers to a
                woman's . . . nether regions.

ADAM/LEWIS   I didn't know the Indians were Dutch.

AUSTIN/CLARK   No, not the Netherlands, the nether regions.

ADAM/LEWIS   So I shouldn't put my finger in a dyke?

                (*Audience groans. Even* REED *and* AUSTIN
                shake their heads in disgust.)

                    (*to audience*) Just wanted to make sure you're
                    all paying attention out there.

AUSTIN/CLARK   I think you owe these good people an apology.

ADAM/LEWIS   I think we owe them their money back. All
                right, all right, I'm sorry. I promise – I will
                never use that word again.

AUSTIN/CLARK   What word?

ADAM/LEWIS   Squaw.

                    (AUSTIN *hits him again. SFX: cymbal crash.*)

AUSTIN/CLARK   I'm sorry about that. But we were also on a
                scientific expedition. We took extensive notes
                of the flora and fauna and sighted many wild
                animals. We saw rattlesnakes . . .

ADAM/LEWIS   They go, "Ssssss!"

AUSTIN/CLARK   We saw grizzly bears . . .

ADAM/LEWIS   They go, "Grrrr!"

AUSTIN/CLARK   We saw wild geese . . .

ADAM/LEWIS   They go, "Squawk!"

                    (AUSTIN *hits* ADAM *again. SFX: cymbal crash.*)

AUSTIN/CLARK   What's the matter with you? Can't you learn
                anything? Didn't you ever go to college,
                stupid?

ADAM/LEWIS   Yeah, but I came out the same way.

                    (*SFX: Slide Whistle. Audience generally reacts
                    negatively.*)

AUSTIN/CLARK   Come on, people, these are the best jokes of
                1805! They don't get any better than this.
                Anyway, we were out on the trail for twenty-

eight months, relying only on the Providence
of God and our native wit.

ADAM/LEWIS   Oh! Clark, Clark! Wait! (*Leaps DC.*) Man goes
into a doctor's office. Says, "Doc, I'm a teepee,
I'm a wigwam. I'm a teepee, I'm a wigwam." Doc
says, "Sit down, you're two tents."

(*SFX: Two horn honks.*)

AUSTIN/CLARK   What was that?

ADAM/LEWIS   Native wit.

(*SFX: About seven cymbal crashes!* AUSTIN *and*
ADAM *turn to* REED.)

AUSTIN/CLARK   What was that?

REED   Heavy cymbalism.

(*SFX: Cymbal crash!*)

ADAM/AUSTIN   Goodnight, everybody! (*They sing.*)

GOOD-BYE EVERYBODY,
BOY WE'RE GLAD TO BE GONE . . .

(*They pull themselves into opposite wings with
their canes, as* REED *quickly strikes the table
to the wings and re-enters.*)

REED   Ladies and gentlemen, Lewis and Clark! Well,
the explorations of Lewis and Clark bring us to
the year 1814, known of course for the War of
1812, remembered chiefly for the British
burning of the White House, and for the birth
of our nation's National Anthem. Francis Scott
Key witnessed the siege of Baltimore from a
neutral ship's cell, where he penned the
immortal words to "The Star-Spangled Banner."

(AUSTIN *enters for a semi-audible conference.*)

AUSTIN   Wait, Reed – I have some problems with "The
                Star-Spangled Banner."

REED   Well, you should explain. (*Exits.*)

AUSTIN   Okay. You're right. Look, don't get me wrong.
                "The Star-Spangled Banner" was a perfectly
                fine song in its day. but it's completely out of
                touch with modern sensibilities. It's militaristic,
                it's patriarchal, and just take a look at the
                musical range.

                (*He turns a new page on the flip chart. "The
                Star-Spangled Banner" is graphed out with no
                regard for musical accuracy.*)

                I mean, it's all over the place. It goes from a
                low B-minus all the way up here to an H above
                high C. And still, Francis Scott Key expects fat
                guys at ball games to sing a song written in the
                key of Q.

                (ADAM *and* REED *[with accordion] re-enter.*)

ALL   We need a new national anthem!

REED   And I think it should be "God Bless America"
                or possibly "Born in the USA".

AUSTIN   Those are both good.

ADAM   Yeah, or "Freebird".

AUSTIN   Well, not "Freebird". "Freebird" was written by
                a Canadian so it's not really appropriate . . .

ADAM   A Canadian? "Freebird" was written by Lynyrd
                Skynyrd. They're from Alabama. (*Realizing.*)
                No, you're thinking of "Snowbird" by Anne
                Murray.

AUSTIN   How does that go?

ADAM   You know . . .

ALL   (*singing*) "Spread your tiny wings and fly away
. . ."

(*They all stare into space and sigh at the
thought of the song's beauty.*)

AUSTIN   Anyway . . . as we're all agreed that we should
have a different national anthem, I've written
my own modest example. Could I get a G?

(REED *hits an extremely sour note on the
accordion.*)

Thank you. Now this is a song which some of
you may recognize. Maestro?

(REED *plays and* ADAM *flips the chart while*
AUSTIN *sings to the tune of "America the
Beautiful".*)

OH, BEAUTIFUL FOR SPACIOUS SKIES
AND NON-EXPLOITED WAVES OF
                        BOTANICAL COMPANIONS
FOR MOUNTED MAJESTIES OF COLOR AND
    FREE-ROAMING NON-HUMAN BEINGS
BESIDE THE DIFFERENTLY-HARVESTED
                                                PLAIN
OH NON-EUROCENTRIC BIO-REGION
NON-THEOLOGICALLY SPECIFIC SUPREME
                    BEING – IF SHE EXISTS
SHED AMBIGENIC GRACE ON THEE
AND MADE YOU MORE
OF A NON-SPECIESISTIC MULTICULTURAL
                                ECO-WARRIOR
FROM CHRONOLOGICALLY-GIFTED
            ANTHROPOMORPHIZED RIVER
TO COSMETICALLY-ENHANCED SEA

(ADAM *turns pages on the flip chart,
displaying the most egregiously multi-syllabic
phrases from the song as* AUSTIN *sings them.
The final three signs say "Austin loves big
words", "It took him three weeks to write*

this", and, at the end, "Applause". AUSTIN
bows and ad-libs "Play ball!" as he and ADAM
exit. Then REED plays "Dixie" on the
accordion.)

REED   The Civil War. North versus South. Industrial
                        versus Agrarian. Madonna versus Shania
                        Twain. Just as Vietnam was the first war
                        broadcast nightly into American homes, the
                        Civil War is the first of which we have actual
                        photographic images. Tonight we are proud to
                        relive the triumph and tragedy of the American
                        Civil War in a slide show entitled, "THE
                        AMERICAN CIVIL WAR: THE SLIDE SHOW."

ADAM   (*re-entering*) Come with us now back in time
                        now to America of the mid-1800s. What was the
                        fuel that stoked the fire that made the steam
                        that drove the engine that was the machine of
                        19th Century American conquest and
                        domination? It was the blood and sweat of
                        Africa. Millions of brothers and sisters lost
                        their lives at the hands of slave traders, and
                        that's no joke. But by 1861 the pressure was
                        building and the engine was about to blow.
                        They called it the Civil War but there weren't
                        nothing civil about it. Now, we're going to
                        need some help from the audience on this one.
                        If anyone here in the audience has a slide
                        projector, please raise your hand.

                        (AUSTIN *and* REED *have re-entered in time to*
                        hear ADAM *asking for a projector.*)

AUSTIN   (*to* ADAM) You were supposed to bring the
                        projector!

REED   (*to* ADAM) Like somebody's going to bring a
                        projector to the theatre.

AUSTIN   What are we going to do? Maybe there's one
                        backstage . . .

(*In the meantime, someone in the front row raises his or her hand.*)

ADAM   Really? you brought one? Can I borrow it? I'll give it right back.

(ADAM *goes to collect the projector.* AUSTIN *and* REED *stare, amazed.*)

ADAM   Hey, I got one!

AUSTIN   That is so cool.

ADAM   You really saved my ass. I owe you.

(*Obviously, the projector has been set in the audience before the show, and the House Manager has warned the lucky person to raise his or her hand at the appropriate moment.*)

(*During the next speech* REED *sets a table down centre for the projector.* ADAM *sets the projector on the table and begins to fiddle with it.* REED *moves the flip chart to just left of upstage centre and flips it to a clean, white page that will act as a screen.* ADAM *motions for* REED *to move it centre so that it is lined up with the projector, which is DC.* REED *misunderstands and takes one deliberate step toward centre.* ADAM *gestures again.* REED *takes another deliberate step.* ADAM *points at at* REED, *then the chart, then repeats that several times so it looks like he's indicating that* REED *should spin in a circle, which* REED *does. Frustrated,* ADAM *moves the chart to centre himself. When he turns to return to the slide projector,* REED *returns the flip-chart to where it originally was – left of centre. This finishes by the time* AUSTIN *says "Mason-Dixon line".*)

AUSTIN   Now while Reed and Adam set up, let me give you a bit of historical background. The importation of slaves into America was

declared illegal in 1807, but the domestic slave
trade continued to grow. Now, the national
debate on slavery was growing, too, and the
Missouri Compromise of 1820, which allowed
slavery in Missouri but nowhere else north of
its southern border, created an actual line
dividing north and south. This was part of the
Mason-Dixon Line, and set the scene for the
war which killed more men named Zeke than
any war in history. So . . . (*It's always nice if
you can use the actual name of the sound
operator here. Makes 'em feel special.*) . . . if
you'll roll the tape, we are proud to present the
sounds and images of that enormous and
devastating conflict, the Civil –

(ADAM *accidentally drags the projector onto
the floor by pulling the chord while looking
for an outlet. It smashes. Slides fly all over the
stage. The three boys desperately attempt to
gather the slides and fix the projector. Over
the loudspeaker Civil War music plays, and a*
WOMAN *and* MAN *begin their dramatic
recorded narration. The boys gesture to the
sound booth to try to get the sound turned off.
When this fails, they decide in a panic to enact
the slides themselves.*)

WOMAN   (*voice over*) The time between the inauguration
                         of George Washington and Abraham Lincoln
                         was only 72 short years. And yet, in those 72
                         years, America had grown into two separate
                         nations.

                         (*Beep.*)

MAN   (*voice over*) The South: agrarian, rich in
                         tradition. The North: progressive and
                         industrial.

                         (*Beep.*)

WOMAN   (*voice over*) For years, these two nations had
                         struggled with one another.

*(Beep. Blackout. By now, they've cleared the
stage of props and exited.)*

MAN   *(voice over)* At the heart of the fighting was
the issue of slavery. And when abolitionist
Abraham Lincoln became President in 1861, the
South seceded from the Union. The Civil War
had begun.

*(Beep. Lights up on the boys dressed as Civil
War soldiers striking an emotional pose.)*

WOMAN   *(voice over)* This photograph, by Civil War
photographer Matthew Brady, captures the
emotion of the Confederate soldiers at the
Battle of Bull Run.

(Beep. Blackout.)

MAN   *(voice over)* The war was the bloodiest in the
history of the nation.

*(Beep. Lights up: Same pose as before except
now* REED *is plunging a knife through* ADAM'S
head.)

Take a moment now to focus the projector . . .

*(The boys shuffle downstage, holding the pose
as best they can.)*

. . . good.

(They stop. Blackout.)

WOMAN   *(voice over)* There was intense and deadly
hand-to-hand combat.

(Beep. Lights up on AUSTIN *kicking* REED *in
the groin. Blackout.)*

MAN   *(voice over)* Occasionally, soldiers had their
legs blown off.

(*Beep. Lights up on* ADAM *standing on one leg holding a dismembered leg. Blackout.*)

WOMAN   (*voice over*) But in the end, the North overwhelmed the South through sheer numbers.

(*Beep. Lights up on* REED *as a Union Soldier with a sign saying "17" and* AUSTIN *as a Confederate with a sign saying "3". They bow. Blackout.*)

MAN   (*voice over*) And so, Robert E Lee finally surrendered at Appomattox, Virginia on April 8, 1865. And they all lived happily ever after. Except for Abraham Lincoln who was shot in the head by John Wilkes Booth and died the next morning.

(*A really long Beep, like an EKG machine flatline when someone is dead.*)

WOMAN   (*voice over*) Inspiring the joke, "But other than that, Mrs. Lincoln, how did you like the play?" Ha, ha, ha!

MAN   (*voice over*) Shut up and stick to the script.

WOMAN   (*voice over*) Oh my, do I detect a note of professional jealousy?

MAN   (*voice over*) It's just not funny!

WOMAN   (*voice over*) You're just threatened because I'm a woman.

MAN   (*voice over*) What if I am, you (*Beep. Beep. Beep.*) and (*Beep.*)? You think you can use me for sex and then treat me any way you want in public!

WOMAN   (*voice over*) I was always honest with you! You knew I could never love you.

*(Beep. Lights up. "The Battle Hymn Of The
Republic" begins to play as* ADAM *enters SL as
an usher in pillbox and epaulettes. He walks
in rhythm all the way across the stage and off
into the wings. He brings on a chair and sets
it DR. He dances balletically to the music.*
AUSTIN *as* JOHN WILKES BOOTH *hops on from the
SL wing and twirls his moustache.* ADAM *turns
quickly to see him, but* AUSTIN *leaps into the
wings. They do this hide-and-seek twice more.
Finally* ADAM *shrugs and turns over a sign on
the flipchart: FORD'S THEATRE – APRIL 14,
1865.* REED *enters in an Abraham Lincoln
Bunraku Puppet suit: a two-foot long neck
connecting to an inflated balloon head with a
happy face crudely drawn on it, Abe Lincoln
beard, and top hat, and five-foot arms with big
hands at the ends. The left hand holds a ticket.*
LINCOLN *waves at the audience, hands* ADAM
his ticket. ADAM takes *the ticket, and directs*
LINCOLN *to his seat DR.* LINCOLN *sits, clapping
in time to the music.* AUSTIN/JOHN WILKES
BOOTH *enters. He is normal-sized, but carries a
huge cut-out of a pistol. He shoots at* LINCOLN.
ADAM *appears again and carries an oversized
bullet on a stick across the stage. It is a large
replica of the bullet used to illustrate the
"shot heard round the world" earlier in the
act. On a musical cue the bullet strikes*
LINCOLN *in the head. The balloon pops,
scattering confetti all over the stage.* REED/
LINCOLN *collapses in his chair.* ADAM *turns the
bullet around revealing a large red 'X'. The
three boys step downstage into three pools of
light and speak conspiratorially.)*

AUSTIN   John Wilkes Booth shot Lincoln in a theatre
                  and ran to a warehouse. Lee Harvey Oswald
                  shot Kennedy from a warehouse and ran to a
                  theatre.

ADAM   Lincoln had a secretary named Kennedy.
                  Kennedy had a secretary named Lincoln.

REED	Three days before he died Lincoln was in Monroe, Maryland. Three days before he died, Kennedy was in Marilyn Monroe.

AUSTIN/ADAM   Whoah!

(The "roe" in Mon-roe and the "Whoah!" rhyme and should be said in unison.)

AUSTIN   And consider this dismaying observation: Ronald Wilson Reagan – how many letters in each name?

REED   Six-six-six. Reagan believed in the rapture and was the first President elected in a zero year not to die in office since William Henry Harrison died in 1841.

ADAM   Not so surprising, Mr and Mrs Bury-My-Head-In-The-Sand, when you consider the role of the Trilateral Commission, the NSC, and the IMF.

AUSTIN   There's a top secret Air Force hangar in Nevada housing an alien spacecraft.

REED   We could be killed for divulging that information.

ADAM   And where exactly was David Duchovny on the day Malcolm X was assassinated?

AUSTIN   Did you know they faked the moon landing on a Hollywood sound stage?

ADAM   Did you know that William Shatner wears a hairpiece?

REED   Did you know that there's a cult of dyslexic devil worshippers in the Ozarks who've sold their souls to "Santa"?

AUSTIN   Do you know the person on your left has to take a leak?

REED   And so do I.

ADAM   And so do I.

AUSTIN   And so do I. Go out to the lobby.

REED   Talk amongst yourselves.

ADAM   Do not make eye contact.

AUSTIN   We'll meet you back here in 15 minutes.

REED   This conversation never happened.

ALL   Shhhhh!

                (*They each put a finger to their lips as the lights fade.*)

                END OF ACT ONE

ACT TWO

In the darkness, battle sounds and music: "Over There".
Lights up. The stage is empty other than three overturned
chairs DC.

ADAM crosses the stage wearing his epaulets from Ford's
Theatre and carrying a sign: I M M. In the middle of the stage
he looks down at the sign and turns it right side up to read:
WW I . As he passes the chairs, ADAM flips the sign over to
read: THE TRENCHES . He exits. REED/SGT and AUSTIN/
COLLEGE BOY run on and jump into a trench somewhere in
France. They carry water rifles and stare grimly out over the
audience. The audience often reacts vocally to the sight of the
water guns. AUSTIN waits to speak until the audience is quiet
– sometimes this takes quite a while.

AUSTIN   It's pretty quiet out there.

REED   Yeah. Too quiet. They've hardly laughed since
               the Civil War.

AUSTIN   I wish Adam would get back.

               (*If you successfuly got an answer from the*
               latecomers back in the Amerigo Vespucci
               scene, you can use it here. After AUSTIN *says* "I
               wish Adam would get back", REED *can respond*
               with "I wouldn't expect him any time soon.
               He's stuck in traffic" – *or out parking the car,*
               having dessert, waiting for the babysitter, lost
               on the freeway or whatever other lame excuse
               your latecomer came up with.)

               How long's he been gone?

REED   Since 1430.

AUSTIN   1430? That's almost 500 hundred years. (REED
               does a slow, incredulous look at AUSTIN.)
               Dammit! I should've gone. Adam's just a kid.
               He doesn't understand the complex, almost
               postmodern irony of a World War fought over
               jingoistic and chivalrous 19th-century ideals

but using 20th-century weapons of carnage and destruction.

REED   You're right – you should've gone. Look, college-boy, the only complexity you need to understand is that we're just prawns in an international cocktail. We're expendable. We got a job to do and we do it. Case closed.

AUSTIN You think they're still out there, Sarge?

REED   They're out there, Shakespeare. Every last one of them. Well, except for that one elderly couple who were offended by the Spiro Agnew/ Grow a Penis joke.

AUSTIN Look, Sarge – it's Adam!

REED   Cover him!

        (ADAM *runs through theatre as* REED *and* AUSTIN *squirt the audience.* ADAM *squirts too, but has only a small water pistol.* ADAM *dives into the trench.*)

REED   What's your report, soldier?

ADAM   Report? Damn!

        (ADAM *has forgotten the report. He runs out into the audience again.* REED *and* AUSTIN *cover him as before.* ADAM *comes right back in.*)

REED   Now what's your report, soldier?

ADAM   Amazing colors on the horizon, sir. Very Impressionistic.

REED   You've been too close to the mustard gas again.

ADAM   Yes, sir. Any movements here?

AUSTIN   Just my own.

REED   Shut up. I think the Krauts are still in position.

ADAM   Let's check it out.

              (ADAM *hands out viewing instruments from his pack*: REED – *binoculars*, AUSTIN – *periscope, and* ADAM – *a ViewMaster.*)

REED   My God.

AUSTIN   We're outnumbered 100 to 1.

ADAM   By animals! There's Bambi and Thumper and Flower, and they're in 3-D!

REED   Gimme that! Use these.

              (REED *grabs* ADAM'S *ViewMaster and hands him the binoculars.* ADAM *looks through them backwards.*)

ADAM   What are we worried about? They're midgets!

              (REED *grabs the binoculars and turns them around.* ADAM *looks through them again.*)

              Oh, my God, they're huge!!

REED   Gentlemen – the brown stuff has hit the blender.

AUSTIN   (*panicking*) I gotta get outa here! I'm too young to die! I got a girl back home . . .

REED   Calm down, soldier.

AUSTIN   Okay.

REED   (*to* ADAM) Now, let's get to business. What did HQ say?

ADAM   Oh right. HQ said, "Your sector surrounded.
                Unable to send reinforcements. Have a nice
                day."

AUSTIN   What are we going to do, Sarge? You got all
                the answers. What are we going to do?

REED   (*slowly*) I don't know. I just don't know. I
                really haven't got a clue. I possess a total lack
                of both ideas and imagination. My ignorance
                on this point verges on the criminal. I don't
                know, I just . . . (*Suddenly optimistic.*) Wait a
                minute! . . . (*Dejected again.*) No. I just don't
                know.

ADAM   I know! We could sneak away in disguise.

REED   Are you kidding? They'll shoot us down like
                clay pigeons.

ADAM   No, not "in the skies", in "disguise"!

REED   Oh, I see.

AUSTIN   There's no way that can work! We might as
                well just eat our guns and order new helmets!

                (AUSTIN *puts his water gun in his mouth.*)

REED   Calm down, soldier! (*Slaps him.*)

AUSTIN   But don't you see?! We're trapped! We're just
                cannon-fodder for the military-industrial
                complex! (REED *slaps him again.*) We're
                doomed! We're gonna die!! I'm never gonna
                see my girl again . . . (REED *kisses him on the
                cheek.*) Thanks. I needed that.

ADAM   I'm telling you, Sarge, this disguise will work!

                (*He starts to pull clothes out of his backpack.*)

REED   I hope those are German uniforms.

ADAM   Better than that – we'll dress up as the
                    Andrews Sisters!

                    (*He pulls out three matching blond wigs
                    attached to military caps, and stuffed bras.*)

REED   But the Andrews Sisters won't be popular until
                    World War II.

ADAM   (*pointing to the audience*) But the Germans
                    don't know that! Come on! Put these on!

AUSTIN   This ain't happenin', man, this ain't happenin',
                    man . . .

REED   (*adjusting his boobs professionally*) Don't
                    worry, Austin, it'll be great. Just like when we
                    were kids.

                    (ADAM *and* AUSTIN *look at* REED.)

                    Didn't you ever dress up like your sister?

                    (ADAM *and* AUSTIN *shake their heads.*)

                    Strap on those boobs, soldier! That's an order!

ADAM/AUSTIN   Yes, sir!

REED   Adjust wigs!

ADAM/AUSTIN   Yes, sir!

REED   How do I look?

ADAM/AUSTIN   Strangely attractive, sir!

REED   All right, men, we're going over the top. Don't
                    stop singing 'til we're marching down
                    Broadway! Professor! Give us the note!

                    (AUSTIN *blows a note on the pitch pipe. They
                    dance and sing beautifully in three-part
                    harmony.*)

ALL   HE WAS A SWEET CONSTRUCTION
                     WORKER OUT OF 'FRISCO BAY
               AND HE WOULD QUITE DIVINELY
                     DANCE THE NIGHT AWAY
               HE WAS A SIGHT IN TIGHT BLUE JEANS
               AND HE WOULD FIGHT FOR WHAT'S RIGHT
               THAT'S WHY HE JOINED THE MARINES
               BUT THEN HE SAID HE'S GAY
               SO HE WAS BLOWN AWAY
               BY THE NERVOUS HOMOPHOBIC BOYS OF
                     COMPANY A!

REED   Lock and load! Let's go!!!

               (*They leap out of the foxhole, shooting. The
               moment they leap the lights flash and the
               sounds of war – horrible machine-guns,
               explosions, whistling bombs – reverberate
               through the theatre. The boys freeze the
               instant they are 'shot'. The lights fade. The
               sound segues into a radio broadcast.*)

AUSTIN   (*voice over*) That was Division 13 of Baker
               Company singing a song that won't be a hit for
               another 30 years. We now return you to the
               plush Starlight Room high atop the Palace
               Hotel for the scintillating sounds of Harry
               Dame and his Band of Acclaim. But first, the
               news. Dateline: 1919. The Treaty of Versailles
               is signed in Versailles. The Great War is over.
               18th Amendment ratified, creating Prohibition.
               And the Golden Age of Radio unites the
               country coast to coast transcontinentally from
               sea to shining sea!

               (*Lights up on the boys at an old-fashioned
               microphone. They all have scripts – perhaps
               each in a different color [red, white, and
               blue?] – and they toss the pages on the floor
               as they finish reading them. ADAM has a guitar
               [or harmonica], and on a music stand a bike
               horn, a slide whistle, and a train whistle.*)

AUSTIN   On in three, two . . .

                  (*He counts "one" silently then points to*
                  ADAM, *who plays three notes on his guitar.*)

ADAM   "You're listening to WXYZ, abridged radio of
                  the 20s, 30s and 40s."

REED/   "Good evening, Mr and Mrs America and
ANNOUNCER   welcome once again to another thrilling
                  adventure of America's Favorite Cowboy
                  Dodge Rambler-Boy Buckaroo. Brought to you
                  by the makers of Thunder Bread – "

                  (AUSTIN *makes the sound of thunder.*)

                  " – yes, Thunder Bread, individually sliced for
                  your convenience with eight essential vitamins
                  that'll make your body big where you need it.
                  Thunder Bread. (*More thunder.*) It'll make your
                  body big where you need it."

                  (ADAM *plays a western tune on guitar.*)

                  "And now, journey with us back to those
                  rugged days of yore, when men were men and
                  so were the women, when frontier justice held
                  sway, and America's Hero, Dodge Rambler-Boy
                  Buckaroo, ruled the west with his best girl
                  Molly and his faithful horse Gordon. Tonight,
                  the makers of Thunder Bread (*Thunder.*) and
                  WXYZ –"

                  (AUSTIN *squeezes a bike horn hidden in the
                  front of* ADAM'S *trousers. Twice.*)

ADAM   What are you doing?

AUSTIN   Nothing. I'm just squeezing that horn you
                  have.

ADAM   No – here's my horn.

(ADAM *picks a bike horn off of the music stand.*)

ALL   EEUUWW!!

REED   "We present Episode 34: 'Dry Days in Dusty Gulch'."

                (ADAM *crows like a rooster.*)

                "A new day dawns in Dusty Gulch, as Dodge helps Molly plan the new schoolhouse."

ADAM/MOLLY   "It sure is good of you to help with the plans for the schoolhouse, Dodge."

AUSTIN/DODGE   "Shucks, Molly, t'ain't nothin' any other red-blooded American Hero wouldn't do."

ADAM/MOLLY   "It's just that you're so busy I'm amazed you have time for little ol' me."

AUSTIN/DODGE   "I always have time for you, Molly."

REED/   "Just then, there came a knock at the
ANNOUNCER   door."

                (ADAM *knocks three times on his guitar.*)

AUSTIN/DODGE   "Come in."

                (ADAM *makes horse noises.*)

AUSTIN/DODGE   "Why, it's Gordon, my faithful and trusty steed. What's troubling you, Gordon?"

                (ADAM *makes more horse noises.*)

AUSTIN/DODGE   "What?! Timmy's trapped on a cliff and needs insulin?!"

                (ADAM *makes a negative-sounding horse noise.*)

AUSTIN/DODGE   "Oh! Bad guys have come to Dusty Gulch?"

                (*An affirmative horse noise.*)

AUSTIN/DODGE   "Molly, you better stay here."

ADAM/MOLLY   "Oh, Dodge, I'm coming with you."

AUSTIN/DODGE   "No, Molly. I don't want you mixed up in this."

ADAM/MOLLY   (*in* DODGE'S *voice*) "But I'm so mixed up
                already."

AUSTIN/DODGE   "Wait, that's my voice!"

ADAM/MOLLY   "See, I told you I was mixed up."

AUSTIN/DODGE   "Then let's go, Gordon, to vanquish those
                ne'er-do-wells!"

                (ADAM *pounds his chest to simulate hoof-*
                beats.)

REED/   "What's the trouble down at the Lucky Shot
ANNOUNCER   Saloon, and why exactly is Adam slapping his
                chest? The answer to these and other
                questions – (*To* ADAM.) knock it off or I'll kill
                you (ADAM *stops slapping his chest.*) – will
                come right after this message from the makers
                of Lucky Stroke Cigarettes. Four out of five
                doctors recommend Lucky Stroke Cigarettes to
                boost their practices. Lucky Stroke. You're a
                Lucky Guy to have a Lucky Stroke. And now
                back to Dodge Rambler-Boy Buckaroo."

                (ADAM *plays a chord on the guitar and then*
                slaps his chest to make the sound of hoof-
                beats.)

                "Dodge and Gordon race down to the Lucky
                Shot Saloon, and burst through the door."

                (ADAM *blows a train whistle.* REED *and* AUSTIN
                look at ADAM *in confusion.*)

REED/ ANNOUNCER	With the Transcontinental Railroad, apparently.
AUSTIN/DODGE	"What seems to be the prob– ?"
REED/JEDGAR	(*using his finger as a pistol*) "Put 'em up, Rambler. We got you covered."
AUSTIN/DODGE	"Who are you?"
ADAM/HERBERT	"Shut up, cowboy, or I'll plug ya full of lead."
REED/JEDGAR	"Well, if it ain't the famous Dodge Rambler- Boy Buckaroo. I 'spect you've heard of us. We're the Hoover Boys – I'm Jedgar, this here's my brother Herbert."
AUSTIN/DODGE	"So you're the infamous Jedgar Hoover. Nice dress."
REED/JEDGAR	"Thanks."
AUSTIN/DODGE	"Dusty Gulch doesn't require your services. Begone."
REED/JEDGAR	"Now hold on, Rambler. We're here to help Dusty Gulch comply with the new federal law."
AUSTIN/DODGE	"What new federal law?"
REED/JEDGAR	"The new Constitutional amendment prohibiting alcohol."
	(AUSTIN/DODGE *laughs long and hard*.)
AUSTIN/DODGE	"No, seriously, what new federal law?"
REED/JEDGAR	"I'm serious, Rambler. Herbert – hold up that newspaper."
	(ADAM *loudly shakes one page of his script to make the sound of a newspaper rustling*.)

REED/JEDGAR   "It says so right here: 'The Eighteenth Amendment to the Constitution prohibits the manufacture, sale, or transportation of intoxicating liquors.'"

AUSTIN/DODGE   "Knock it off, Herbert, or I'll run you in."

ADAM/HERBERT   "Oh, yeah? On what charge?"

AUSTIN/DODGE   "Rustling."

(If the audience really groans at this, REED *says "Sounds like there's a wind storm a-brewin'.")*

(ADAM *stops rustling.*)

REED/JEDGAR   "And so the gentle folk of Dusty Gulch are forced into hiding as the hideous Hoover Boys sweep through town, sucking up all that is decent and good."

(ADAM *and* AUSTIN *both make a huge sucking sound.*)

AUSTIN   "Hmm, that was good."

ADAM   "And decent."

REED   "Meanwhile, Dodge Rambler-Boy Buckaroo and his faithful horse Gordon bunk down under the Dusty Gulch sky as night falls."

(Slowly, one by one, AUSTIN *chirps like a cricket,* ADAM *hoots like an owl,* REED *howls like a coyote,* ADAM *hoots and screeches like a monkey.* AUSTIN *and* REED *look at* ADAM *disapprovingly, then* REED *puts his hand to his mouth and makes a fart sound.* AUSTIN *and* ADAM *look at* REED *in disgust and fan away the odor with their script pages.)*

AUSTIN/DODGE   "Well, Gordon, another day gone and this
                Prohibition law isn't working. If only we could
                find out who's behind it!"

                (ADAM *makes sound of horse snorting.*)

                "Gordon! Are you sure?!"

                (ADAM *again makes the sound of a horse
                snort.* AUSTIN *has come to the bottom of his
                page. He drops it on the floor and reads from
                the top of the next page.*)

                "Errot era eenum woe?" (*He stares at the page
                in confusion. It's upside down. He turns it
                right-side up and reads it again.*) "How many
                are there?"

                (ADAM *stomps his foot three times.*)

                "Oh, Gordon – you're the best hero an
                American horse ever had. Let's ride! We've got
                a Prohibition to prohibit."

                (ADAM *strikes a chord on the guitar and then
                slaps his chest to simulate the sound of horses
                galloping.*)

REED/   "Undaunted, Dodge dashes desperately down
ANNOUNCER   to Dusty Gulch to detect the deadly and
                drunken desperadoes and detain them
                indefinitely in the dark and dirty dock of
                destiny, and other 'D' words."

                (ADAM *makes the sound of a horse whinny,
                then honks the bike horn.*)

AUSTIN/DODGE   "So – Al Capone. We meet at last."

ADAM/CAPONE   "How'd you know I was here, Rambler?"

AUSTIN/DODGE   "I got it from the horse's mouth. Come on,
                Capone, I'm taking you in."

REED/J EDGAR	"Not so fast, Rambler." (*Points his pistol/ finger at* AUSTIN.)
ALL	"Gasp!"
AUSTIN/DODGE	"Jedgar!"
ADAM/MOLLY	"Dodge!"
AUSTIN/DODGE	"Molly!"
REED/J EDGAR	"Capone!"
ADAM/CAPONE	"Rosebud!"
REED/JEDGAR	"Drop your guns, Rambler, or the girl gets it."
AUSTIN/DODGE	"You'll never get away with it, Jedgar!"
ADAM/CAPONE	"Oh, I think we will."
REED/JEDGAR	"Say goodbye to your lady, Rambler."
AUSTIN/DODGE	"No, wait! Do what you want with the girl but let me go!"
REED/JEDGAR	"All right."
ADAM/MOLLY	"Dodge, no!"
REED/ ANNOUNCER	"Suddenly, over the hills in a cloud of dust and the sound of a thundering wheelchair, appears Franklin Delano Roosevelt!"
AUSTIN/FDR	My fellow Americans, the only thing we have to fear is fear itself. Of course, as fears go, that's a pretty big one. Still, we must not let ourselves get down. To illustrate this, I'd like to read a letter from little Amy in Warwickshire. She writes: "Dear FDR, Germany's acting up again. I'm scared. Can you help us? Your fan, Amy." Well, Amy, this is the kind of letter that pisses Americans off! Our country's in a

Depression but we will beat it! I'm going to
create the WPA, the CCC's, the TVA . . .

(*With a slide whistle,* ADAM *makes the sound
of a radio tuning. At the same time,* REED
mimes turning the tuning knob on a radio.)

REED/
ANNOUNCER

Twelve years later . . .

(ADAM *makes the radio tuning sound again,
and* REED *mimes changing stations again.*)

AUSTIN/FDR

. . . the FBI, the FDIC, and the IUD. We hereby
declare war on the axis powers. Oh, Lucy, come
rub my aching . . .

(REED *makes a "Click" sound and mimes
changing the station.*)

REED/
ANNOUNCER

". . . back to the exciting conclusion of Rock
Fury, Super GI."

(*The boys march in place.*)

AUSTIN/
ADOLPH

"Oh, my darling Eva, look! Ze allies are
marching into Berlin. Zey are falling right into
my trap. Now I will press zis button, firing the
secret Uberveapon zat vill vipe out ze whole
Allied force. Ha-ha-ha-ha!"

(*Marching stops.*)

ADAM/EVA

"Oh, Adolf, I love it ven you're in a syphilitic
rage!"

(ADAM *makes a "WOOSH" sound, the sound of
a man flying.*)

AUSTIN/
ADOLPH

"Ach, my little shnitzel-gruber – vait. Vut is zat
noise? Oh, no! It's a bird, it's a plane . . ."

(REED *makes a short "spurt" noise. Then*
AUSTIN *wipes an imaginary bird dropping out
of his eye.*)

AUSTIN/ ADOLPH	"Oh, it's a bird."
REED/ROCK	"No! It's Rock Fury-Super GI! Your jig-dancing days are over little man."
AUSTIN/ ADOLPH	"But vy? Vy?!"
REED/ROCK	"Vy? I'll tell you vy. In its greed and lust for power, Germany has tried to take over an entire continent."
ADAM/EVA	"But isn't zat vut ze US did in Norze America?"
REED/ROCK	"Wash your mouth with soap, little lady! Why, we stopped land-grabbing over forty years ago. And there's a big difference between your land-grabbing and ours."
AUSTIN/ ADOLPH	"Vut's zat?"
REED/ROCK	"We succeeded. Besides, we didn't try to wipe out an entire race of people!"
ADAM/EVA	"Vut about ze Indians?"
REED/ROCK	"Well, we don't lock people away in concentration camps."
ADAM/EVA	"Vut about ze Japanese-Americans on ze Vest Coast?"
REED/ROCK	"You know, it's lucky for you, ma'am, I don't hit women."
	(ADAM *claps his hands once to simulate the sound of a slap.*)
ADAM	"Ow."

REED/ROCK	"Much. Now let's go. If I had to hazard a guess I'd say that you two will be spending more than 12 years in Leavenworth."
AUSTIN/ ADOLPH	"Or 11 years in Twelvevorth."
ADAM/EVA	"Or five and ten at Voolvorth's."
REED/ROCK	"That's enough. Now give me your gun and let's go."
AUSTIN/ ADOLPH	"Here's my Lugar pistol."
	(AUSTIN's *gun is his index finger and thumb. He "hands" it to* REED.)
REED/ROCK	"I've always wanted to see one of these. Is this the safety?"
	(REED *shoots twice at* ADOLPH *and* EVA.)
ADAM/EVA	"BANG!"
AUSTIN/ ADOLPH	"BANG!"
ADAM/EVA	"Ugh!"
AUSTIN/ ADOLPH	"Ugh!"
REED/ROCK	"Oops. Well, thank goodness we won this war, otherwise . . ."
AUSTIN/ HAWKEYE	"Help, help!"
REED/ROCK	"Wait – my super-hearing is picking up Alan Alda calling for help in Korea. Rock Fury-Super GI is off once again to battle for truth, justice, and American markets."

(AUSTIN *and* ADAM *make a "WOOSH!" to indicate* ROCK FURY *flying away.* ADAM *then makes a news-ticker sound underneath:*)

AUSTIN   This just in – Atom Bombs dropped on Hiroshima and Nagasaki. Over 200,000 dead. That report in just a moment, but first it's time to play *Queen for a Day*!

ADAM/REED   (*lamely*) Yay.

AUSTIN   The game show which celebrates the achievements of American women, and where an ordinary housewife, a lowly homemaker, a societally-conditioned domestic slave, can become *Queen for a Day*!

ADAM/REED   (*lamely*) Yay.

AUSTIN   Just by proving her knowledge of feminist history. Or should I say herstory? Reed?

REED   Thank you, Austin. But before we play our game we need a female volunteer, a lovely little gal from the studio audience to come up here on stage and clean up this terrible mess that we've made. Any volunteers?

ADAM   Now before you raise your hand, we're looking for someone who's used to being bossed around and told what to do like all the time.

(REED *and* AUSTIN *look at* ADAM.)

ADAM   That's me, isn't it?

(AUSTIN *exits while* ADAM *begins to clear the stage.*)

REED   Okay, let's play *Queen for a Day*. Today's first question – if you think you know the answer, raise your hand. Who was the most famous female American anarchist/organizer of the

early 20th Century, founder of Mother Earth
magazine, and lover of Sasha Berkman?

(AUSTIN *re-enters with a cardboard paper
towel tube to use as a microphone. He goes
out into the audience.* REED *raises his hand as
he says this to demonstrate . . .and to
discourage the audience from yelling out the
answers.*)

AUSTIN   Look at all the hands shooting into the air.
Everyone wants a piece of this question.
Here's a lovely lady. (AUSTIN *approaches an
actual woman audience member.*) Tell me,
dear, what's your name and where are you
from? (*She tells him. He repeats her name and
home town.*) Tell me, dear, do you know the
answer to Reed's question? (*She will rarely
know the answer, so* AUSTIN *helps her.*) That's
okay. Nobody goes away empty-handed. I'll
give you a hint. Just say, "Emma Goldman".

1ST VOLUNTEEER Emma Goldman.

AUSTIN   Emma Goldman, Reed?

REED   (*reading the answer from the page of his radio
script*) No, I'm sorry the answer is Whoopie
Goldberg.

AUSTIN   I'm sorry, very close. But just for playing our
game we'd like to present you with this:
Number One in our series of Great American
Women Trading Cards. Collect all three!

(*If the audience boos,* AUSTIN *says,* "That is
exactly the right response.")

REED   Oh, we're awfully progressive here in the
1950s, aren't we, Austin?

AUSTIN   We sure are, Reed. Blame it on Mamie
Eisenhower, I say. Here is a woman who . . .

(He describes and names the woman on the actual card, some great woman from American history, such as Susan B Anthony, Harriet Tubman, or Elizabeth Blackwell. Then he presents the card to the audience member. We used actual cards from a "Famous American Women" card game that is now sadly out-of-print. But what the heck – make your own!)

Thank you very much for playing our game. A big hand for the little lady right here!

(REED leads the audience in applause. AUSTIN dashes up and around to the back of the theatre.)

REED   Okay, let's go to question two. Remember, get it right, become Queen for a Day. This one's a little easier. Name the brave seamstress from Montgomery, Alabama, who refused to move to the back of the bus and jump-started the American civil rights movement.

AUSTIN   Brave seamstress, civil rights movement. Well, here's a lovely lady. Tell me, dear, what's your name, where you from? *(She tells AUSTIN her name and town.)* Well, first of all . . . *(her name)*, I want to thank you for speaking directly into my cardboard microphone so everyone could hear you. Tell me, dear, do you know the answer to Reed's question?

2ND VOLUNTEER   Rosa Parks?

                (You'd be amazed, but some people actually don't know this. Or they panic and can't remember. Whichever, they deserve to be chastised. AUSTIN can say, "Really?" and then announce "The (name of her city) School System, ladies and gentlemen!" Then he can take pity and tell her: "You know you should know this, don't you? I'll give you a hint. Just say 'Rosa Parks'.")

AUSTIN   Rosa Parks, Reed?

REED   (*again reading the answer*) No, I'm sorry. The
                  answer I have here is Whoopie Goldberg.

AUSTIN   Oh, too bad. I think she played her in the
                  movie. But just for playing, here's Number Two
                  in our series of Great American Women Trading
                  Cards. Here is a woman who . . . (*He describes
                  and names the woman on the actual card, then
                  presents it to the volunteer.*) Thank you very
                  much for playing our game! A big hand for the
                  little lady right here!

                  (*Again,* REED *leads applause.* AUSTIN *moves
                  down to the front of the audience.*)

REED   Well, no winner yet, but we still have question
                  number three. Austin, if they get this right,
                  what will they win?

AUSTIN   Well, Reed, the person who answers this
                  question correctly will win Number Three in our
                  series of Great American Women Trading
                  Cards: that ground-breaking veterinary brain
                  surgeon – Zira from Planet of the Apes. Reed?

                  (REED *looks quizzically at* AUSTIN, *who
                  shrugs.*)

REED   Okay. Here's the final question: Name the first
                  female ever elected to the United States House
                  of Representatives.

AUSTIN   Oh, everybody's thinking, 'I should know this I
                  should know this.' Let's see, here's a lovely
                  lady. Tell me, sir, what's your name? (*This time*
                  AUSTIN *has selected a man as the volunteer.
                  The guy says his name.*) And where are you
                  from? (*The guy says the name of his town.*) I'm
                  sorry? (*He repeats the name of his town.*) No, I
                  heard you. I'm just sorry.

(AUSTIN *and* REED *laugh hysterically, out of all proportion to the quality of the joke.* ADAM *re-enters and joins in.*)

AUSTIN   Ah, the old ones are the best ones, aren't they
              . . . (*The guy's actual name*)? As we've been
              proving all night. Tell me, do you know the
              answer to Reed's question?

3RD VOLUNTEER Whoopie Goldberg?

AUSTIN   Whoopie Goldberg is correct!

              (AUSTIN *hands him the card and leads the
              applause*[1]. *After* AUSTIN *gives away the Zira
              card, he attempts to go on.*)

AUSTIN   Okay, ladies and gentlemen, we've covered a
              lot of material very quickly, so if you have any
              questions about American history now would
              be the time –

              (But REED *and* ADAM *look into the wings as if
              the stage manager is signaling to them.* ADAM
              whispers into REED'S *ear and exits.* REED *tries
              to interrupt* AUSTIN.)

REED   (*to audience*) Austin? Austin? (*To audience.*)
              Excuse me.

              (*He whispers in* AUSTIN'S *ear.*)

AUSTIN   What? No he's not.

_____

[1] About half the time, the guy actually doesn't say 'Whoopie
Goldberg'. AUSTIN can prompt him by saying, "Would you like
to make a guess based on the previous two questions?" With
any luck this time the guy answers 'Whoopie Goldberg' and
you can move on. But if the guy still doesn't know, AUSTIN will
ask the audience what the answer is and they will invariably
respond, 'Whoopie Goldberg!' If it's gone this far, AUSTIN tears
the card into pieces and tosses them into the air for the
audience to share.

REED	Adam says he's here.
AUSTIN	Well, he's fooling you.
REED	Probably. Let me check.

(REED *runs backstage.*)

AUSTIN	Someone's pulling your leg.
REED	(*off*) Ohm my gosh! Yes! He's here!

(AUSTIN *turns to the audience, unsure of how to continue.*)

AUSTIN	Um . . . change in plan. Apparently, we have a very special guest here tonight. Just arrived from Washington DC on Air Force One, give a big welcome to President George W Bush.

(REED *enters as Bush, wearing a cowboy hat.* ADAM *enters behind him as a Secret Service agent.*)

AUSTIN	Mr President, it's an honour to have you here. We were just about to take questions from the audience about American history. (*As if someone in the audience just suggested this.*) Oh! That's a great idea. We have a tremendous opportunity, ladies and gentlemen. Now that he's here, you can ask President Bush any question you have about American history, his policies, anything you want. So be thinking of some questions. I'll start. Mr President, why are you here?
REED/BUSH	I would like to undress your audience.
AUSTIN	You'd like to *address* the audience?
REED/BUSH	That's what I said.
AUSTIN	Please, go ahead.

REED   (*with many Bush-like pauses*) Thank you for
                        this inopportunity. You know, when I first ran
                        for President, the American people had a
                        choice. They decided they were fed up with
                        business as usual. They were tired of hanky-
                        panky in the Oval Office and scandals like
                        Whitewater and Travelgate. there were fed up
                        with a booming economy and budget
                        surplusses. And they were sick of the United
                        States cooperating with its allies and the UN to
                        keep peace in the world. I am reminded of the
                        great Ronald Reagan who in 1980 asked the
                        American people are you better off today they
                        they were four years ago. I'd like to thank you
                        for ignoring that question and re-electing me to
                        a second term.

                        (AUSTIN *smiles at the answer, looks at the
                        audience, then responds.*)

AUSTIN   Okay. Wow. Well, let's throw it open here.
                        Who has a question for the president? Raise
                        your hand. Who wants to start?

REED/BUSH   Bring 'em on.

                        (*They take three to five questions from the
                        audience.* AUSTIN *always repeats the question
                        after the audience member has asked it so that
                        everyone can hear it and also to buy* REED *a
                        little time to think of an answer. If at first
                        nobody raises a hand, get the ball rolling.*)

AUSTIN   Okay, I'll start. Mr Bush, why were the early
                        American settlers called Yankees?

REED/BUSH   Why were they called Yankees? That's easy.
                        Because there were very few women among
                        them.

                        (*Take a few questions from the audience.
                        Don't let it go on too long.* AUSTIN *then says:*)

AUSTIN

Wow. These are great questions. I have one that I'm sure everyone else is wondering about, too. Mr President, boxers or briefs?

REED/BUSH

(*shrugging, confused*) Boxers. Briefs. Depends.

(AUSTIN *finds a man near the front.*)

AUSTIN

Hey, did you hear what this guy said? Man, this isn't like TV. I can hear you, too.

(REED *and* ADAM *break out of character.*)

REED

I didn't hear what he said.

ADAM

He said we've left out 50 years of history.

REED

What 50 years?

AUSTIN

Oh, I know – you're talking about the 50 years between the Civil War and World War I, right?

REED

Well, did it ever occur to you that we left it out on purpose because it wasn't a very funny time in American history?

ADAM

No, he said we left it out because we don't know anything about it. And I'm almost positive I heard him say that you're bald.

(*Hair-length differs from actor to actor. Actual baldness may vary. You may want to come up with a different insult here, one that matches your actor's most obvious physical trait.*)

(AUSTIN *and* ADAM *restrain* REED *from beating the crap out the guy.*)

REED

Oh, man, that's it! I don't have to put up with that!

AUSTIN

Yeah, but we should answer the guy's question.

REED	You want to answer his question after he's been rude?
AUSTIN	He's American. He can't help being rude.
REED	Okay, we'll answer the question but it's going to be short, okay, because it wasn't a very funny time in American history. Here it is. There was labor unrest . . .
ALL	Not funny.
REED	There was land-grabbing on an unprecedented scale . . .
ALL	Not funny.
REED	There were seven-year olds working themselves to death in sweatshops.
ALL	. . . well, that's pretty funny, actually . . .
AUSTIN	That covers everything up to the end of World War II, doesn't it?
ADAM	Shall we move on?
REED	Yes. Great questions, give yourselves a big round of applause.
	(AUSTIN *and* ADAM *exit.*)
REED	We now move on to the final chapter of the History of America, in which myriad events collide and deflect, each seeming significant yet disjointed. And how better to capture the spirit of post-war America than with –
AUSTIN	(*entering*) – a medley of Broadway show tunes!
	(AUSTIN *begins singing a show tune. But* REED *and* ADAM *[who's re-entered] cut him off.*)

REED   Austin, we are not doing Broadway show
                        tunes!

AUSTIN   I thought we agreed. The Broadway musical is
                        America's greatest contribution to world
                        theatre!

REED   No, the world knows post-war America through
                        the hard-boiled detective. It's the film noir
                        ending.

AUSTIN   No, not the film noir ending.

ADAM   Austin, you are such a dick! We voted . . .

AUSTIN   I changed my mind.

ADAM   You can't change your mind on a vote! Okay,
                        we'll vote again. This time we'll use the
                        audience. (AUSTIN *disagrees*, REED *agrees*.)
                        Let's do this by applause. Everyone in favor of
                        Austin's stupid Broadway ending, applaud.
                        (ADAM *leads the applause*.) Everyone in favor
                        of Reed's thoughtful film noir ending?
                        (*Inevitably,* AUSTIN *wins the audience vote*.)
                        Well, it looks like Austin wins the popular
                        vote.

AUSTIN   Thank you. (*Starts to go*.)

REED   (*looking at the page of radio script that he is
                        still holding – it also had the "Queen For A
                        Day" questions on it*) And we win in the
                        Electoral College!

                        (REED *and* ADAM *slap hands and celebrate*.)

AUSTIN   NO!!! All right, all right! I'll do the film noir
                        ending, but only if I get to play all the good
                        parts: Conspirator Guy, Lt Flush, Richard
                        Nixon, Ronald Reagan.

REED   Fine.

ADAM	What do you mean "fine"? What do I get to play?
REED	All the women.
ADAM	Yeah! Cool.
	(ADAM *and* AUSTIN *exit*.)
REED	Okay, post-war America, film noir ending. Play it – (*You can use the name of the actual sound operator here, again.*)
	(*Film noir-style music plays: a slow jazz number.* REED *dons an overcoat and fedora which* ADAM *has already set on the microphone stand.* REED *then strikes the stand and steps into a pool of light.*)
REED/SPADE	The name's Diamond, Spade Diamond. My friends call me Spade Diamond. I'm a private eye. The phone in my office had been gathering dust for weeks when a beautiful redhead walked in.
	(ADAM *walks in dressed like Lucille Ball in "I Love Lucy".*)
ADAM/LUCY	Hello, Spade.
REED/SPADE	Lucy Ricardo, what are you doing here?
ADAM/LUCY	I know I shouldn't have come, Spade, but I need your help.
REED/SPADE	Sure, now you need my help. But five years ago you ripped my heart out like it was a blue chip stamp to stick it into another man's coupon book.
ADAM/LUCY	Well, if you won't help me maybe your brother Neil will.
REED/SPADE	I wouldn't bet on it.

ADAM/LUCY	Why not?
REED/SPADE	He's been dead for three years.
ADAM/LUCY	Oh, my God. Look, Spade. I know it's none of my business and you might just tell me to shut up, but what happened to your brother?
REED/SPADE	Shut up, Lucy. It's none of your business that my brother Neil was a second-rate Hollywood actor who got labeled a communist, blacklisted, and committed suicide.
ADAM/LUCY	I'm sorry I asked.
REED/SPADE	(*to audience*) Just then my hand rang. Brrring!
	(REED *uses his hand like a phone.* AUSTIN/ CONSPIRATOR GUY *appears in a pool of light across the stage. He wears thick, coke bottle glasses.*)
REED/SPADE	Hello?
AUSTIN/ CONSPIR GUY	If you know what's good for you, you'll drop this case before you start it. Unless you want to find out the truth about your brother.
REED/SPADE	My brother? (*To audience.*) I decided to trace the call. I had to keep him talking. (*To* AUSTIN/ CONSPIRATOR GUY.) Hello, I'm tracing this call and need to keep you talking. Who is this?
AUSTIN/ CONSPIR GUY	Just call me the Conspirator Guy.
REED/SPADE	The Conspirator Guy? Whaddaya know about my brother?
AUSTIN/ CONSPIR GUY	Sorry. Gotta go. Click.

(AUSTIN/CONSPIRATOR GUY *drops a card on the stage and exits.*)

REED/SPADE   He'd stayed on the line just long enough. I traced the call to a pool of light on the far side of the stage.

(REED/SPADE *crosses the stage and picks up the card.*)

REED/SPADE   "The Conspirator Guy. For more information dial 411. This will count against your minutes." (*Turns card over.*) "Hanoi Hilton at midnight." Sorry, Lucy, gotta go.

ADAM/LUCY   Wait, Spade. You can't leave me like this! Ricky's being investigated by a government committee tomorrow. We think it's because he's Cuban and there's this Cold War on. Waahh!!

REED/SPADE   Look, Lucy, McCarthy and his cronies mean business. They're only gonna let Ricky go if you give 'em a scapegoat.

ADAM/LUCY   A scapegoat?

REED/SPADE   That's what I just said. Somebody to blame instead of Ricky. (*Shaking her.*) Who's it gonna be, Lucy? Think! Think!

ADAM/LUCY   I know! Fred and Ethel!

REED/ McCARTHY   Fred and Ethel who?

ADAM/LUCY   Our landlords, Fred and Ethel Rosenberg.

REED/SPADE   It's so crazy . . .

BOTH   It just might work.

AUSTIN/RICKY   (*off*) Lucy! Lucy! You got some 'splainin' to do!

ADAM/LUCY   I'd better go, Spade. I got some 'splainin to do.

                 (ADAM *plants a big "Bugs Bunny Kiss" on*
                 REED *and runs off.*)

REED/SPADE   I felt strange stirrings. I knew Lucy would take
                 care of herself. It was one of two things she did
                 very well. Now I had to get to Hanoi.

                 (REED *mimes steering a car.* AUSTIN/FLUSH
                 enters.)

AUSTIN/FLUSH   Hold it, Diamond. Stop milking that cow!

                 (REED/SPADE *is momentarily confused, then
                 realizes that his "car steering" looks like
                 "cow milking".*)

REED/SPADE   (*to audience*) It was Lt. Flush, SFPD. He'd
                 been trying to nail me for years. (*To* AUSTIN.)
                 Whaddaya want, Flush? I'm a busy man.

AUSTIN/FLUSH   You still haven't explained your connection to
                 those maternity ward bombings.

REED/SPADE   Maternity ward bombings? You got the wrong
                 guy. You can't connect me to the Baby Boom.

AUSTIN/FLUSH   Oh, yeah?

REED/SPADE   Yeah. Why don't you go chase a real criminal
                 like Tony the Tiger?

AUSTIN/FLUSH   I'm not after serial killers, Diamond, I'm after
                 you!

REED/SPADE   Well, when you find something that'll stick in
                 court, besides your underwear, give me a call.

                 (REED *drives away downstage.* AUSTIN *walks
                 backward upstage and off, facing* REED *and
                 calling after him the whole time. The illusion*

is that REED *is driving away and leaving* AUSTIN *behind.*)

AUSTIN/FLUSH   (*calling*) I'll get you, Diamond . . . ! (*Exits.*)

REED/SPADE   I had to get to the Hanoi Hilton. I took a left turn up Market Street, past the Golden Gate Bridge . . .

(ADAM *crosses upstage with a painted cardboard cut-out of the Golden Gate Bridge.*)

The Statue of Liberty . . .

(AUSTIN *crosses upstage dressed as the Statue of Liberty.*)

And the Texas Book Depository . . .

(ADAM *crosses upstage with the famed "bullet marked with an 'X'" on a stick.*)

. . . that bullet sure gets around. I knew the Hanoi Hilton. It was the seediest of the seedy in a town known for seeds, seediness, and horticulture of all types. And like Dorothy Parker said, you can lead a whore to culture but you can't make her think. And I should know. (*Audience boos.*) Get over it. Conspirator Guy?

(AUSTIN/CONSPIRATOR GUY *has entered as the audience booed. He sets two chairs down and sits on one of them.*)

AUSTIN/
CONSPIR GUY   Hello, Spade.

REED/SPADE   Thanks for the invite. What can you tell me about the Cold War and how it relates to the Domino Theory, Vietnam, and my brother?

AUSTIN/
CONSPIR GUY   It's all an elaborate game with one side trying to keep the other in check. The Domino Theory says that if Vietnam goes communist, the rest

of Asia will fall to the Reds one by one, like
dominoes.

REED/SPADE   You mean they'll deliver in 30 minutes or less?

AUSTIN/   Not any more. They had that lawsuit,
CONSPIR GUY   remember . . . ?

(ADAM *saunters on in a slinky black dress,
sunglasses, and black beret.*)

ADAM/JO   Hello, tall, dark, gruesome. Buy you drink?

REED/SPADE   I wouldn't say no.

ADAM/JO   I'll be right back. (*Exits.*)

REED/SPADE   (*to audience*) She was the most beautiful
              woman I'd ever seen. I wanted to make love to
              her in the worst way – standing up in a
              hammock.

(*As the audience laughs,* AUSTIN/CONSPIRATOR
GUY *seems puzzled.*)

REED/SPADE   What are you doing?

AUSTIN/   I'm just trying to picture that.
CONSPIR GUY

REED/SPADE   Knock it off! Who is she?

AUSTIN/   Jo Chi Minh. Daughter of the leader of North
CONSPIR GUY   Vietnam. She'll have some answers but be
              careful, Spade, she's trouble.

REED/SPADE   Dry up and blow away.

AUSTIN/   Okay. It's your bar mitzvah.
CONSPIR GUY

ADAM/JO   Pucker up and blow.

(AUSTIN/CONSPIRATOR GUY *exits, as* ADAM/JO
enters.)

REED/SPADE   So, Jo – whaddaya know?

ADAM/JO   Not much. Here your drink.

REED/SPADE   Thanks. So what's with this war, sweetheart?

ADAM/JO   Why you want know?

REED/SPADE   Just trying to clear up some family business.

ADAM/JO   Family business, eh? Speaking family business,
                 remind me of little story. When I small child,
                 rice paddies Vietnam, I be walking . . .

                 (REED/SPADE *talks over* ADAM/JO.)

REED/SPADE   (*to audience*) The longer she spoke, the more I
                 realized that Adam had no idea how to do a
                 Vietnamese accent.

ADAM/JO   No, I don't really. But question to you, Mr So-
                 called Spade: Are you on their side or our side?

REED/SPADE   I'm on my own side.

ADAM/JO   Oh, I see.

REED/SPADE   So where were we?

ADAM/JO   The roar. (*"Roar" is* ADAM'S *bad-accented
                 pronunciation of "war".*)

REED/SPADE   Right. The roar. Look, I need some answers and
                 I need 'em now: Why is the US so interested in
                 a little country in southeast Asia? It doesn't
                 make sense.

ADAM/JO   Ah, but it does. Who stands benefit from war?
                 Figure that out, Mr Diamond, you home free.
                 Look! Another monk is setting hisself on fire!

> (REED/SPADE *looks away in the direction*
> ADAM/JO *is pointing.* ADAM/JO *pours*
> *something into* SPADE'S *drink.*)

REED/SPADE   A monk on fire? I don't see a monk on fire.

ADAM/JO   Oh, he must have gone out. Don't make monks
              like they used to. Well, cheers.

REED/SPADE   Here's looking at you, kid.

ADAM/JO   Over the lips, past the gums. Look out tummy,
              here it comes.

REED/SPADE   Up yours.

ADAM/JO   Up yours, too.

> (REED/SPADE *drinks and suddenly grabs his*
> *throat. He passes out.* ADAM/JO *exits, striking*
> *the two chairs. Colored lights flash. Hard*
> *Rock music from the '60s blares over the*
> *speakers. We hear JFK say, "Ask not what*
> *your country can do for you" then the BANG*
> *of a gunshot. Then Martin Luther King: "I*
> *have a dream!" BANG! Malcolm X: "By any*
> *means necessary." BANG! RFK: "To follow in*
> *the footsteps of my brother." BANG! Anne*
> *Murray: "Spread your tiny wings and fly*
> *away." BANG! In the middle of these*
> *voiceovers,* REED/SPADE *has slowly and*
> *unsteadily gotten to his feet.*)

REED/SPADE   Whatever she slipped me, it was strong. I was
              high all right, and I'm not talking vertically. I
              saw two figures approaching me. At first
              glance, they looked like Neil Armstrong and
              Buzz Aldrin.

> (ADAM *and* AUSTIN *walk towards him in slow-*
> *motion, as if they were walking on the moon.*
> AUSTIN *wears a military cap.* ADAM *wears an*
> *oversized Uncle Sam hat.*)

AUSTIN	This is one small step for man, one giant leap for mankind.
REED/SPADE	But as they got closer they looked more like Ken Kesey and Timothy Leary.
ADAM	Tune in, turn on, drop out!
REED/SPADE	Where am I?
AUSTIN	You're having an hallucination.
REED/SPADE	Who are you?
ADAM/SAM	I'm Uncle Sam. Uncle Sam-I-Am. Do you like my war in Vietnam?
REED/SPADE	I do not like your Vietnam. I do not like it, Sam-I-Am.
ADAM/SAM	Are you fond of Lyndon Johnson? Did you like the Gulf of Tonkin, Operation Rolling Thunder, Flaming Dart, or the Mai Lai blunder?
AUSTIN/TOUGH	The kids at home align with Mars, Burning draft cards burning bras. Do you like the riots in the inner cities? Did you think Kent State was pretty?
REED/SPADE	I did not like the riots in the inner cities. I did not think Kent State was pretty. I do not like this drugged-out dream. I do not like your rhyming scheme. I do not like your Vietnam. I do not like it, Sam-I-Am.
ADAM/SAM	Are you fond of Agent Orange? Do you . . . ? Damn!
REED/SPADE	I had him trapped. There is no rhyme for orange. (*To* AUSTIN.) Okay, Buckwheat, what's the bird's-eye lowdown?

AUSTIN/TOUGH   Not so fast, Diamond. We got a couple of
               questions for you. Where was Lucy Ricardo on
               the day JFK was assassinated?

REED/SPADE   (*to audience*) So, Kennedy was dead and they
               were trying to blame it on Lucy. I had to think
               quick. (*To* AUSTIN.) She was with me.

ADAM/SAM   She couldn't have been with you, Diamond,
               'cause we were following you that day.

REED/SPADE   She was with me, but she was disguised.

AUSTIN/TOUGH   So, Lucy was disguised with Diamond.

               (*Audience groans. All three actors do a slow
               take to the audience.*)

REED/SPADE   (*to audience*) You're right. I should've seen
               that one coming. (*To* AUSTIN.) Look, act like a
               couple of good boys and take a long walk off a
               short dwarf.

AUSTIN/TOUGH   (*menacingly*) That's good, Diamond. But I'm
               afraid we're gonna have to rough you up.

REED/SPADE   No!

ADAM/SAM   Yeah.

REED/SPADE   (*to audience*) Sensing an opportunity, I
               slammed my face into his fist.

               (*Clown-like,* AUSTIN *rapidly punches* REED'S
               face like a punching bag. REED *reacts
               appropriately, spits out dry white lima beans
               like fake teeth, screams, and then passes out
               on the floor. Blackout. Lights up.*)

REED/SPADE   When I came to, I was in the Watergate Hotel.

AUSTIN/NIXON   (*he enters speaking into his wrist-watch*)
               Tricky Dick to Checkers. Tricky Dick to

Checkers. Come in please. I am not a crook. Repeat. I am not a crook. And let me make one thing perfectly clear. (*Shakes his jowls.*)

REED/SPADE   It was former Vice-President Nixon, one of the biggest commie-hunters of his time.

AUSTIN/NIXON   That's President Nixon now, son. And commie-hunting is passé. In fact, I'm using détente to open relations with the Soviet Union and Red China. (*Speaking into watch.*) Watergate to White House, Watergate to White House, come in please.

REED/SPADE   You mean the Cold War is over?

AUSTIN/NIXON   No, sir. The Reds are still our mortal enemies but we'd like them to be our pals as well. There's a lot of untapped potential there. Untapped. Get it? Heh-heh. Must be a Democrat. Rrring! (NIXON *answers his watch.*) Hello? It's for you.

REED/SPADE   (REED *speaks into* NIXON'S *watch*) Hello? (REED *listens to the watch as* AUSTIN *garbles something inaudible, in the* CONSPIRATOR GUY *voice, into his sleeve.* REED *speaks again into the watch.*) I'll be there. So long. (*To* NIXON.) I gotta go. Happy tapping. Hey, do that Nixon salute for me before you go.

AUSTIN/NIXON   Aw, what the heck.

(NIXON *strikes the double victory-sign pose and dashes offstage. Blackout, then lights up on* REED.)

REED/SPADE   I was told to meet a contact at the corner gas station. On the way there I heard that Nixon had resigned the Presidency but landed on his feet, whereas just the opposite had happened to Gerald Ford. When I got to the gas station there was a line a half-mile long and I had to

wait over an hour to get gas. I looked for my
contact.

(ADAM *enters dressed as an* ARAB, *holding a
newspaper with two hands*.)

ADAM/ARAB   Pssst!

(ADAM/ARAB *gestures with his head for* REED/
SPADE *to approach him. A third hand reaches
over the top of the newspaper and hands* REED/
SPADE *a note. [NB:This magic trick is
available at most magic shops.]* ARAB *exits*.)

REED/SPADE   Thanks. (REED/SPADE *turns away, then stops
when he realizes the* ARAB *had three hands.
He looks back, then shrugs. Continues cross
downstage*.) "Dear Spade: Have been called to
Iran to release some hostages. If you want
more information, go to the White House, ask
for Ronald Reagan." Ronald Reagan? The only
Ronald Reagan I knew was an actor who
starred in "Bedtime for Bonzo". That's absurd.
The American people couldn't be that gullible.

(*Lights up on* AUSTIN *as* REAGAN, *shrugging his
shoulders in that familiar way*.)

AUSTIN/REAGAN   Well . . . I, uh . . . well . . .

(ADAM *enters as* GEORGE BUSH. *He hands a
clear jar of jellybeans to* AUSTIN.)

ADAM/BUSH   Here's your breakfast, Mr President.

AUSTIN/REAGAN   Thank you, Nancy.

ADAM/BUSH   I'm not Nancy. I'm your Vice President –
                 George Bush.

AUSTIN/REAGAN   George Bush? I loved you in *Oh God*.

ADAM/BUSH   I wasn't in *Oh God*. You're thinking of George
                 Burns.

AUSTIN/REAGAN	You're George Burns?
ADAM/BUSH	No – George Bush.
AUSTIN/REAGAN	Really? I used to have a Vice President named George Bush.
ADAM/BUSH	That's me.
AUSTIN/REAGAN	Well, you look just like him.
ADAM/BUSH	(*consulting clipboard*) Okay Mr President, we've got a busy day. In fifteen minutes we'll have brownies and milk. Then at noon we invade Grenada.
AUSTIN/REAGAN	Say, that's swell.
ADAM/BUSH	1.15 – cartoons.
AUSTIN/REAGAN	Smurfs!
ADAM/BUSH	Then at two o'clock we're going to fire Donald Regan.
AUSTIN/REAGAN	We're gonna fire me?
ADAM/BUSH	No, Donald Regan.
AUSTIN/REAGAN	Well, that's me – Ronald Reagan.
REED/SPADE	Ronald Reagan?
AUSTIN/REAGAN	See, he knows. (*To* SPADE.) Come in, how are you . . .
REED/SPADE	The name's Diamond. Spade Diamond. I'd like to ask you a few questions.
AUSTIN/REAGAN	Okay. As I said to John Hinckley, fire away. Heh-heh!
REED/SPADE	Do you believe in the Domino Theory?

AUSTIN/REAGAN   Oh, yes. Mommy and I love to play dominoes
                 while we drink hot cocoa and watch *The
                 Waltons*.

REED/SPADE   No, the Domino Theory of international
                 communism.

AUSTIN/REAGAN   Well, I . . . uh . . .

ADAM/BUSH   We're doing everything we can, Mr President.

AUSTIN/REAGAN   We're doing everything we can, Mr President.

REED/SPADE   Were you behind the October Surprise?

AUSTIN/REAGAN   I don't recall.

REED/SPADE   As President of the Screen Actors' Guild did
                 you blacklist my brother?

AUSTIN/REAGAN   I don't recall.

REED/SPADE   Did you order Oliver North to trade arms for
                 hostages?

AUSTIN/REAGAN   You bet your ass, buddy . . .

                 (AUSTIN/REAGAN *falls immediately asleep,
                 standing up.*)

ADAM/BUSH   Why don't you ask me? I am the ex-director of
                 the CIA.

REED/SPADE   What can you tell me about the Cold War?

ADAM/BUSH   Fightin' it in the Middle East. Stayin' the
                 course. Movin' forward. Soviet communists in
                 Afghanistan. Bad people. Baa-aad. Installed
                 the Shah to keep out the communists. But that
                 Ayatollah Khomeini threw him out. And that's
                 bad.

REED/SPADE   What are you doing about it?

ADAM/BUSH	Found some friends there. Gonna help us out. We're sendin' money and weapons to our good buddies Osama Bin Laden and Saddam Hussein.
REED/SPADE	Never heard of 'em.
ADAM/BUSH	Don't worry. You will.

(ADAM/NANCY *makes the sound of a phone ringing and answers it.*)

ADAM/BUSH	Hello? What? Drunk again? (*To* SPADE.) Thank goodness I kept George W out of Vietnam. He coulda hurt somebody over there. (*Listening to phone again.*) What's that? Okay, I'll tell him. And remember, stay the course. Thousand points of light! (*He hangs up.*)
REED/SPADE	Who was that?
ADAM/BUSH	Bill Casey over at the CIA wanted me to pass on a message from the Conspirator Guy. If you want to solve the mystery of the Domino Theory and find out the truth about your brother, meet him at the Berlin Wall, 7.30, checkpoint Charlie.
REED/SPADE	Well, I'd better go. Thanks for the help.

(AUSTIN/REAGAN *wakes as* SPADE *exits.*)

AUSTIN/REAGAN	It's morning in America.
ADAM/BUSH	I'm glad he's gone.
AUSTIN/REAGAN	Who's gone, Nancy?
ADAM/BUSH	George Bu – George Bu – Bu –

(*Frustrated, he segues into imitating a screaming monkey.*)

AUSTIN/REAGAN   Ooh, Bonzo! Bonzo! It's bedtime, Bonzo!

                 (*Blackout. Lights up on* REED/SPADE *in a pool of light.*)

REED/SPADE   I had to get to the Berlin Wall. It seemed appropriate that I was going to crack this case at the Iron Curtain, the dividing place between East and West. Now I had to find a way to get to Berlin.

AUSTIN/FLUSH   (*entering*) I got you now, Diamond! You're dead meat. Your butt is mine. Your ass is grass. Your keister's cooked. Your heinie's history!

REED/SPADE   Calm down, Flush. I don't have time for a long list of rump references.

AUSTIN/FLUSH   You'll be singing a different tune soon, sister, in Sing-Sing. I can prove you're the sick and twisted pervert responsible for . . . Disco.

REED/SPADE   Better watch your backbeat, flatfoot, throwing around accusations like that. You can't connect me to Disco.

AUSTIN/FLUSH   Oh, yeah? What's your favorite kind of music?

REED/SPADE   Disco.

AUSTIN/FLUSH   Gotcha!

REED/SPADE   Damn! I've got to get to Berlin, and you're not gonna stop me!

                 (REED/SPADE *starts running. After a few steps he runs in place.* AUSTIN/FLUSH *takes off after him.*)

REED/SPADE   He was catching up with me. I hopped onto my Harley-Davidson motorcycle.

                 (REED *hops on an imaginary motorcycle and drives DS.* AUSTIN/FLUSH *hops up on his motorcycle, siren blaring. They jockey for position.*)

AUSTIN/FLUSH   Pull over, Diamond!

REED/SPADE   No way!

(REED *accelerates away, leaving* AUSTIN *behind.* AUSTIN *catches up, pulling alongside.* REED *jumps behind* AUSTIN, *as if riding on the back of the same bike.* REED *puts his index finger, like a gun, to* AUSTIN'S *temple.*)

REED/SPADE   Get me to Berlin, and quick!

AUSTIN/FLUSH   Berlin? On a motorcycle? Are you crazy?

REED/SPADE   Don't make any false moves, let's go!

(*They drive around the stage and end up facing the SR wings.*)

REED   (*pointing SR*) Look out! Look out!

AUSTIN/FLUSH   What?

REED/SPADE   A FRUIT STAND!

(AUSTIN *and* REED *scream.* ADAM *runs on from SR and throws a large box of plastic fruit at them, then exits SR.* AUSTIN *and* REED *drive to face stage left.*)

REED/SPADE   (*pointing SL*) Look out! Look out!

AUSTIN/FLUSH   What?

REED/SPADE   A NURSERY SCHOOL!

(AUSTIN *and* REED *scream. Eight or ten baby dolls fly at them from the SL wings.* AUSTIN *and* REED *drive in a circle, ending up centerstage, facing SR.*)

REED/SPADE   (*pointing SR*) Look out! Look out!

AUSTIN/FLUSH   What?

REED/SPADE   THE ATLANTIC OCEAN!!

(AUSTIN *and* REED *scream.* ADAM *runs on from SR and throws a bucket of water on* AUSTIN, *then exits SR.*)

REED/SPADE   (*pointing SR*) Look out! Look out!

AUSTIN/FLUSH   What?

REED/SPADE   THE ENGLISH CHANNEL!!

(AUSTIN *and* REED *scream.* ADAM *runs on again from SR and douses* AUSTIN *with another bucket of water.* ADAM *exits SR.*)

REED/SPADE   (*pointing SR*) Look out! Look out!

AUSTIN/FLUSH   What?

REED/SPADE   ITALY!

(AUSTIN *and* REED *scream.* ADAM *runs on again from SR and bombards* AUSTIN *with spaghetti.* ADAM *exits SR.*)

REED/SPADE   (*pointing SR*) Look out! Look out!

AUSTIN/FLUSH   What?

REED/SPADE   BAVARIA!

(*They start to scream, then stop.*)

AUSTIN/FLUSH   What's wrong with Bavaria?

REED/SPADE   BAVARIAN CREAM PIE!

(AUSTIN *and* REED *scream.* ADAM *enters SR, creams* AUSTIN *with a pie and exits SR.*)

REED/SPADE   (*pointing SR*) Look out! Look out!

AUSTIN/FLUSH   What?

REED/SPADE   THE MOSCOW STATE CIRCUS!

                  (AUSTIN *and* REED *scream.* ADAM *enters SR in a*
                  clown costume. He acts likes he's going to
                  throw the contents of the bucket on AUSTIN
                  and REED, *but then goes to the DS edge of the*
                  stage and throws a bucket of confetti into the
                  audience. He exits SR.)

REED/SPADE   Wait a minute! The Moscow State Circus?
                  We've gone too far.

AUSTIN/FLUSH   You'll never get away with it, Diamond.

REED/SPADE   Oh, I think I will. I just rode a motorcycle
                  across the Atlantic Ocean, didn't I?

AUSTIN/FLUSH   Good point.

REED/SPADE   Back this thing up!

                  (*They make five beeping sounds as they back*
                  up, then dismount.)

BOTH   Berlin!

                  (ADAM/UNCLE SAM *enters SR.*)

ADAM/SAM   Yes! But the Wall is down, the Cold War is
                  over.

REED/AUSTIN   Uncle Sam!

ADAM/SAM   You know too much, Spade. I'd like to
                  introduce you to a friend of mine.

                  (ADAM *reveals the infamous magic bullet with*
                  the 'X' on it, hidden behind his back.)

REED/SPADE   No, Sam! No!

ADAM/SAM   Bonsai!

                  (ADAM *runs toward* REED, *to hit him with the*
                  bullet.)

AUSTIN/FLUSH   Get behind me, Spade! I'll protect you!

                  (AUSTIN *jumps in front of* REED *and takes the*
                  bullet. AUSTIN *collapses,* ADAM *exits, with*
                  REED *shooting at him with his index finger.*)

REED/SPADE   Bang! Bang! Bang! (*Kneeling.*) Hang in there,
                  Flush! Don't die on me, pal! You're gonna be
                  okay!

                  (AUSTIN *raises his head, wearing the*
                  CONSPIRATOR GUY'S *thick glasses.*)

AUSTIN/   Hello, Spade!
CONSPIR GUY

REED/SPADE   Conspirator Guy?

AUSTIN/   That's right. I'm a split personality. Just like
CONSPIR GUY   Jekyll and Hyde. Anne Heche. But before I die,
                  I want to tell you – your brother wasn't a
                  communist. I set him up just like I set up Ricky
                  Ricardo.

REED/SPADE   I knew it! My brother was innocent!

AUSTIN/   And you want to know who caused the Cold
CONSPIR GUY   War? Who benefited?

REED/SPADE   Yes!

AUSTIN/   The Generals!
CONSPIR GUY

REED/SPADE   The military?

AUSTIN/   No, no. General Motors. General Dynamics.
CONSPIR GUY   General Electric. They caused the Cold War!
                  And – I shot JFK, not Lee Harvey Oswald!

REED/SPADE	Really?!
AUSTIN/ CONSPIR GUY	Yeah. I shot Bobby Kennedy, too. And Martin Luther King. And Malcolm X.
REED/SPADE	Wow.
	(*He works himself into a frenzy as he drags himself downstage.*)
AUSTIN/ CONSPIR GUY	And I poisoned Marilyn, and walked on the moon, and burglarized the Watergate hotel . . .
REED/SPADE	Okay!
AUSTIN/ CONSPIR GUY	. . . and I shot JR, and invented the AIDS virus, and I whacked Nancy Kerrigan on the knee, and I'd whack her again if I had half a chance . . .
REED/SPADE	Shut up!
AUSTIN/ CONSPIR GUY	. . . and I made Oprah skinny and then fat again, and I shrank the bloody glove so it wouldn't fit O J anymore, and I told President Clinton, "Go ahead! She's an intern! Who cares?" (*These last two or three confessions change, depending on what's in the news.*)
REED/SPADE	BANG! (*Shoots the* CONSPIRATOR GUY *with his index finger*).
AUSTIN/ CONSPIR GUY	(*with his last gasp*) . . . Schwarzeneggar!
	(AUSTIN/CONSPIRATOR GUY *dies.*)
REED/SPADE	I had to put him out of my misery. So there it was. I'd cracked the case. The Cold War was over, and I had no more answers than when I started. Communism was dead . . . well, except for a billion people in China, and a few hundred million in Vietnam, Cuba, North Korea, Angola,

Mozambique, North Yemen, and Vermont. But
with the fall of the Soviet Union we had no
more enemies. America stood as the lone super
power, admired by all. It was a new world order.
Peace would reign. I needed a drink.

(ADAM/LUCY RICARDO *runs in, out of breath.*)

ADAM/LUCY   Hey, Spade! Forget about the new world order.
                 I need your help!

REED/SPADE   What's wrong, Lucy?

ADAM/LUCY   Ricky went back to Cuba and now he's being
                 held at Guantanamo Bay. They say it's because
                 of this new war on terror.

REED/SPADE   Don't worry, we'll get him a lawyer.

ADAM/LUCY   No, he can't have a lawyer. They're not
                 following the Geneva Convention..

REED/SPADE   Who aren't?

ADAM/LUCY   Colin Powell, Dick Cheney, George Bush.

REED/SPADE   Aren't those the same guys who fought the
                 last war?

AUSTIN/   (*suddenly waking up*) No, you're thinking of
CONSPIR GUY   "Snowbird" by Anne Murray!

                 (REEDSPADE *and* ADAM/LUCY *shoot* AUSTIN/
                 CONSPIRATOR GUY *together. He flops back
                 down.*)

REED/SPADE   Don't worry Lucy, I'll get to the bottom of this.

ADAM/LUCY   But how?

REED/SPADE   As a beautiful woman once asked me, who
                 stands to benefit from the war? We figure that
                 out and we're home free.

ADAM/LUCY	You know, Spade, this new world order seems an awful lot like the old world order.
REED/SPADE	(*to audience*) It looked like that drink was going to have to wait.
	(*They turn and exit. A sign on* ADAM'S *back says "THE END."*)
	(*Lights up as the guys run back on.*)
REED	Thank you. Thank you. Shut up, ladies and gentlemen! That was the Complete History of America. We hope you enjoyed the show. (*To* AUSTIN *and* ADAM.) Is there anything we need to add here historically?
AUSTIN	Nope, we did it all.
ADAM	Well, we left out a few people. Like Jimmy Hoffa.
AUSTIN	He's not that important.
ADAM	Well, not as an individual, but he was symbolic of the labor movement.
AUSTIN	Nah, that's too complex. You can't think of Jimmy Hoffa in the abstract. You need to think of him in the concrete.
ADAM	Yeah, I guess you're right. In that case, I just wanna say that we might have sounded kind of cynical tonight about America and that wasn't our intention. There are a lot of things we love about America and I'd like to mention a few of them now: Sean Connery, the Beatles, and Canada.
REED	Great! Now, we've covered about 50,000 years of American history tonight – war, pestilence, assassination – but you've been a fabulous audience and you don't really deserve to have the show end on such a down note. So, in the

great tradition of American optimism, we would
like to bring you . . .

ALL   . . . a happy ending!

                         (*A rousing patriotic song plays in the
                         background. Lights fade to the three specials
                         from the end of Act One.*)

REED   Tonight we've told the timeline of American
                         history from left to right.

AUSTIN   Past to present.

ADAM   Then to now.

REED   But now we'd like to go backwards in time.
                         Right to left.

AUSTIN   Present to past.

ADAM   Now to then.

REED   And as we move backwards in time, we see the
                         ozone layer growing, the national debt
                         shrinking . . .

AUSTIN   . . . the number of AIDS cases decreasing . . .

REED   . . . and the rain forest growing back at the rate
                         of a thousand acres a day.

AUSTIN   As we move backwards in time, on September
                         11, 2001 we see the World Trade Centre rise
                         from the ashes and tower proudly over
                         Manhattan.

ADAM   We see Michael Jackson getting blacker and
                         blacker.

REED   As we move backwards in time, we see Monica
                         Lewinsky go 'up' on the President.

ADAM   December 7 1941: A day that will live in "famy"
              as the Japanese restore the American fleet at
              Pearl Harbor.

REED   1929: White Wednesday. Stock Market soars to
              new heights, as thousands of people fly to the
              top of tall buildings on Wall Street.

AUSTIN   1874: The National Rifle Association disbands.

ADAM   1775: King George removes tea tax.

REED   1604: Slave trade disappears.

AUSTIN   1500s: Europeans return tons of gold and
              treasure to the Native People of America.

ADAM   1492: Columbus sews the hands back onto a
              quarter of a million Arawak Indians and backs
              his ship up from the New World to Spain.

REED   Finally, the last people walk backward across
              the Bering Strait from Alaska into Asia . . .

AUSTIN   As the North American continent sinks
              peacefully into the sea . . .

ALL   And they all live happily ever after *before*.

ADAM   I'm Adam.

REED   I'm Reed.

AUSTIN   I'm Austin.

ALL   And we're history! Good night!

              (*Blackout. Lights up. The boys bow, come
              together, bow, high-five, and exit.*)

AUTHORS' NOTE

Any scholarly work is dependent on the research of underpaid graduate students, and The Complete History of America (abridged) is certainly no exception. The list below, though well-typed, is by no means complete: in our attempt to grasp some ephemeral notion of truth, we scoured more texts and rare primary sources than we had the energy or attention span to count. The books below are a mere sampling of the wealth of knowledge available to the casual historian, and from which we gleaned* many valuable insights.

The Complete History of America (abridged) is the result of years of scholarship, innuendo, and over-the-counter narcotics. Any resemblance to historical fact is strictly coincidental.

SELECTED READINGS

Barry, Dave: *Dave Barry Slept Here – A Sort of History of the United States*. New York: Fawcett Columbine, 1989. This thin book speaks volumes about the current state of the American educational system.

Brogan, Hugh: *The Penguin History of the United States*. London, 1976. An informative look at America from the unusual perspective of the penguin.

Chomsky, Noam: *Year 501 – The Conquest Continues*. Boston: South End Press, 1993. (Pop-Up Picture Series) This powerful revisionist work would have you believe, among other things, that genocide is a bad thing.

Dahmer, Jeffrey: *Serial Killer Color & Story – An Activity Book for Children*. Milwaukee: Son of Sam Imprint, 1991. A bright and cheerful introduction to some colorful American misfits. Ages 2-7.

Davis, Kenneth C: *Don't Know Much About History*. New York: Crown Publishers, Inc, 1990. A compulsively readable overview of American history from soup (the first Thanksgiving) to nuts (the current administration).

* stole

Diamond, Neil: *The Jazz Singer*. All three formats. A biting and incisive look at the American immigrant experience. (See also Spielberg, Steven: An American Tail.)

Disney, Walt: *Song of the South*. VHS/Beta/Laserdisc. A biting and incisive look at American slavery.

Gaines, William C, ed: *MAD Magazine*. The "Star Blecch!" issue. An important cultural reference. (See also "The Poop-Side-Down Adventure" issue.)

Hamlin, Harry: *LA Law – My Favorite Episodes* (The Complete Scripts). Los Angeles: Full Court Press, 1990. A biting and incisive look at American jurisprudence.

Hoff, Benjamin: *The Tao of Pooh*. New York: Dutton, 1982. Zen for morons.

Kerouac, Jack: *On The Road*. The classic chronicle of soul searching and experimentation that defined a generation. (See also Cassidy, David: *On The Road, Too: My Years on The Magic Bus with the Partridge Family*.)

Loder, Kurt: *Lewis & Clark Unplugged*. New York: MTV Publishing, Inc, 1991. Manifest Destiny goes acoustic.

Murray, Anne, as told to Loder, Kurt: *Snowbird – The Anne Murray Story*. Toronto: Bantam Paperbacks, 1984. The uplifting story of Canada's favorite songbird.

Seuss, Dr: *The Cat in The Hat*. New York: Beginner Books, 1958. The searing and explosive book that first dared to expose the horrors of Vietnam. Ages 2-7.

Shenkman, Richard: *Legends, Lies, & Cherished Myths of American History*. New York: Harper & Row, 1988. Yoko brought a walrus, there was magic in the air.

Shenkman, Richard: *I Love Paul Revere, Whether He Rode Or Not*. New York: Harper & Row, 1990. He more or less didn't.

Spelling, Aaron: *Buying Your Daughter A Career*. Beverly Hills, 90210: Vanity Press, 1991. The struggle for acceptance and respect in a place they call . . . Hollywood.

Tocqueville, Alexis de: *Democracy in America*. New York: Alfred A. Knopf, 1945. Did you know this book was written in the nineteenth century? We didn't.

Tucker, Robert C, ed: *The Marx-Engels Reader*. New York: W.W. Norton & Company, 1972. (Large-Print Edition) Recently discovered radio scripts featuring Groucho, Chico, Harpo, and Friedrich.

Zinn, Howard: *A People's History of the United States*. New York: Harper Perennial, 1980. This subtle understated work makes a pretty convincing case that there's corruption in government. Who knew?

(You may insert this into the programme if you wish.)

THE COMPLETE HISTORY OF AMERICA (ABRIDGED)

Are you getting it all? Don't despair! Tonight, you will have the opportunity to ask us any question you have about American History!

Below are examples of questions we've been asked in the past. We hope they inspire reflection and self-examination (doctors recommend at least one a month). Ask away!

SAMPLE QUESTIONS

1. What was the Society of Cincinnati? An 18th-century group which endorsed an hereditary presidency.

2. What did the Know-Nothing Party stand for? They opposed immigration and Catholics in office; unwilling to divulge this, their response to questions was "I don't know."

3. Was Lincoln a Democrat or a Republican? Republican.

4. What's the difference between the Federalist Papers and the Articles of Confederation? The Papers explained the Constitution and urged its ratification; the Articles predated it and served as the nation's first binding constitution.

5. Which two Presidents died on the same day? Thomas Jefferson and John Adams both died on July 4, 1826.

6. What was Seward's Ice Box? Alaska.

7. In whose administration was Elvis Presley an agent for the Drug Enforcement Agency? Richard Nixon's.

8. When was the Era of Good Feelings? From 1817 to 1825. James Monroe was president and there was only one political party: the Democratic-Republican Party.

9. What does E Pluribus Unum mean? "Out of many, one."

10. What did the Nineteenth Amendment do? Not adopted until 1920, it gave women the right to vote.

11. Who was Harriet Tubman? An abolitionist, spy, and escaped slave who made 19 trips back to the South to lead over 300 slaves to freedom along the Underground Railroad.